THE AMERICAN NEGRO
HIS HISTORY AND LITERATURE

THE
NEGRO AT WORK
IN NEW YORK CITY

George Edmund Haynes, Ph.D.

ARNO PRESS and THE NEW YORK TIMES
NEW YORK 1968

General Editor
WILLIAM LOREN KATZ

GILBERT OSOFSKY, IN HIS BIBLIOGRAPHICAL ESSAY IN HARLEM: *The Making of a Ghetto, Negro New York, 1890–1930* (1966), makes the following brief evaluation of George Edmund Haynes's *The Negro at Work in New York City: A Study in Economic Progress* (1912):

> [It] originated as a Columbia University doctoral dissertation. Haynes later became a Negro leader of national prominence. His information on nineteenth-century economic life is sketchy, but his detailed material on Negro employment and small business in the early twentieth century, often derived from personal investigation and interviews, is enlightening.

There is a reason for the sketchiness of this book on nineteenth-century Negro economic life. As is clear from Osofsky's essay, the only sources on the nineteenth-century New York Negro when Haynes wrote his book were the various U. S. and New York State census volumes, New York Ctiy departmental reports, a few other statistical surveys and newspaper articles, and some sociological canvasses done by church organizations. The many published articles on the New York Negro in the nineteenth century which are listed in Osofsky's book and Seth M. Scheiner's *Negro Mecca: A History of the Negro in New York City, 1865–1920* (1965) have all been written or made available since 1912.

On the other hand, there was a plethora of magazine articles on the twentieth-century New York Negro published before 1912.

These articles, used extensively by Haynes, plus his own personal investigation and interviews, make his book quite solid on the twentieth century.

In Part I Dr. Haynes deals with the Negro as a wage earner; the various occupations open to Negroes in New York over the decades under the general headings of domestic and personal service, trade and transportation, and manufacturing and mechanical pursuits. Part II deals with the Negro in business in New York City—the character of Negro business enterprise, the volume of business, etc. Most of these enterprises grew out of domestic and personal service occupations (groceries, barber shops, restaurants, lodging houses, undertakers, tailor and dressmaking shops, saloons, coal, wood and ice companies, etc.).

Haynes concluded that in domestic and personal service the Negro was poorly paid compared with the cost of living. Where unions admitted him to skilled occupations with wages equal to white workers, the Negro had to be above average in speed, in quality of work done and in reliability, in order to secure and hold these jobs. Southern-born or West Indian Negro businessmen in New York City were handicapped by the denial of chances to get experience in order to be more efficient, had difficulty securing capital and building credit, and were limited to the low purchasing power of Negro patronage by a prejudiced public. Dr. Haynes's report is a story of progress in the face of great adversity.

Ernest Kaiser
SCHOMBURG COLLECTION
NEW YORK PUBLIC LIBRARY

STUDIES IN HISTORY, ECONOMICS AND PUBLIC LAW

EDITED BY THE FACULTY OF POLITICAL SCIENCE OF COLUMBIA UNIVERSITY

Volume XLIX]   [Number 3

Whole Number 124

THE NEGRO AT WORK IN NEW YORK CITY

A Study in Economic Progress

BY

GEORGE EDMUND HAYNES, Ph.D.

Sometime Fellow of the Bureau of Social Research,
New York School of Philanthropy ;
Professor of Social Science in Fisk University

New York
COLUMBIA UNIVERSITY
LONGMANS, GREEN & CO., AGENTS
LONDON: P. S. KING & SON

1912

PREFACE

THIS study was begun as one of the several researches of the Bureau of Social Research of the New York School of Philanthropy, largely at the suggestion of Dr. Samuel McCune Lindsay, the director, to whose interest, advice and sympathy its completion is largely due. Sincere thanks are due the Bureau for making the investigation possible.

The material was gathered between January, 1909, and January, 1910, except about four weeks in August, 1909, during the time that I was pursuing studies at the School of Philanthropy and at Columbia University.

The investigation necessarily involved many questions concerning the personal affairs of many Negroes of New York and it is a pleasant duty to acknowledge the unvarying cheerfulness with which they rendered assistance in securing the facts.

I wish to acknowledge especially the help of Dr. William L. Bulkley in making possible many of the interviews with wage-earners, of Dr. Roswell C. McCrea for criticism and encouragement in preparation of the monograph, and of Dr. E. E. Pratt, sometime fellow of the Bureau of Social Research; Miss Dora Sandowsky for her careful and painstaking tabulation of most of the figures. They should not be charged, however, with responsibility for any of the errors that may be detected by the trained eye.

The study as now published is incomplete. Part I, the Negro as a Wage-earner and Part II, the Negro in Business, were to be supplemented by Part III, the Negro in the Professions. But the time absorbed in gathering the material for the first two parts prevented the securing of a sufficient amount of personally ascertained data for the third; it seemed best to concentrate on the first two for the sake of thoroughness.

The summaries following the data on the several points and at the end of each chapter, and the conclusion at the end of the volume contain some repetitions which may be open to criticism, but they have been retained with the hope of making the monograph useful to those who wish to know the conclusions from the succession of figure upon figure and percentage upon percentage, without necessarily going through these details. At the same time, anyone who may wish to weigh the inferences in the light of the facts has the details before him.

Conditions among Negroes in Philadelphia have been adequately studied in the work of Dr. W. E. B. DuBois and Dr. R. R. Wright, Jr. - It is to be hoped that some time soon the need of similar inquiries in other cities—East, West, North and South—may be realized and that provision may be made in this way for the guidance of the growing impulses of those who wish to better conditions in urban centers.

I am aware that there are good reasons for criticism of these pages. But what has been done was done in the search for the truth, that the enthusiasm of reform may be linked with the reliability of knowledge in the efforts to better the future conditions of the city and the Negro.

GEORGE EDMUND HAYNES.

FISK UNIVERSITY, NASHVILLE, TENN., APRIL 1, 1912.

TABLE OF CONTENTS

PART I

THE NEGRO AS A WAGE EARNER

CHAPTER I

CHAPTER II

CHAPTER III

GENERAL CONDITION OF WAGE-EARNERS

CHAPTER IV

OCCUPATIONS OF WAGE-EARNERS

CHAPTER V

WAGES AND EFFICIENCY OF WAGE-EARNERS

PART II

THE NEGRO IN BUSINESS IN NEW YORK CITY

CHAPTER I

THE CHARACTER OF NEGRO BUSINESS ENTERPRISES

CHAPTER II

THE VOLUME OF BUSINESS

CHAPTER III

DEALING WITH THE COMMUNITY

CHAPTER IV

SOME SAMPLE ENTERPRISES

PART I

THE NEGRO AS A WAGE EARNER IN NEW YORK CITY

PART I

THE NEGRO AS A WAGE EARNER IN NEW YORK CITY

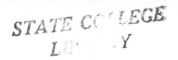
CHAPTER I

THE CITY[1] AND THE NEGRO—THE PROBLEM

THE city of to-day, the growth of the past century, is a permanent development. Dr. Weber has effectively treated the history, nature, causes and effects of the concentration. He shows[2] that the percentage of urban population has varied in different countries; and that this is due mainly to the varying density of population and to the diverse physical features of the countries which have been differently affected by the Industrial Revolution and the era of railroads. The causes of this concentration have been the divorce of men from the soil, the growth of commercial centers, the growth of industrial centers, and such secondary and individual causes as legislation, educational and social advantages.

In the United States, city growth has been affected by all of the several causes that have operated in other countries, modified at times and in places by exceptional influences.[3]

In the discussions concerning the Negro and his movement cityward, it is often assumed that his migration is affected by causes of a different kind from those moving other populations; or that it is not similar in respect to the movement of the white population under similar conditions; or that the concentration can result only in dire disaster

---

[1] The most comprehensive study of city growth is *The Growth of Cities in the 19th Century*, by A. F. Weber, vol. xi, *Columbia University Studies in History, Economics and Public Law* (New York, 1899), pp. 1-478. The meaning of city and urban population is that used by Weber: An agglomerated population of two thousand to ten thousand for towns, more than ten thousand for cities, more than one hundred thousand for great cities. *Cf.* p. 16.

[2] See footnote at the end of this chapter. Weber, *op. cit.*, pp. 146-154.

[3] Weber, *op. cit.*, pp. 167-68; 173-74; 201-207. See also footnote at end of chapter.

both to himself and to the community into which he moves. Such facts as are available suggest that these assumptions are ill-founded. The efforts that are being put forth to improve rural conditions and to advance agricultural arts among Negroes are highly commendable and effective. The thesis of this chapter is that, notwithstanding improvements resulting from these efforts for rural districts, wherever similar causes operate under similar conditions, the Negro, along with the white population, is coming to the city to stay; that the problems which grow out of his maladjustment to the new urban environment are solvable by methods similar to those that help other elements of the population.

In the first place, so far as we know now, the general movement of the Negroes, speaking for the South, does not seem to have been very different from that of the whites. Professor Wilcox says,[1]

It is sometimes alleged that the migration to cities, which has characterized nearly all countries and all classes of population during the last half century, has affected Southern whites more than Southern negroes, and that the latter race is thus being segregated in the rural districts. That such a movement may have gone on, or may now be in progress, in parts of the South can neither be affirmed nor denied on the basis of the present figures, but it may be said with some confidence that, as a general statement applied to the whole South, it is not correct. To be sure the negroes constitute 32.6 per cent of the population of the country districts in the entire South and only 30.9 per cent of the city population, but an examination of the figures (Census 1900) for the several divisions and states will show that what is in some degree true of the South as a whole is not true of most of its parts.

Therefore, it is of importance to note that the movement of white and Negro populations toward cities tends to be coincident. We may get some indication of these movements of white and Negro populations cityward by compar-

[1] Twelfth Census, *Bulletin 8, Negroes in the United States*, p. 29.

ing the growth of their numbers in the principal Northern and Southern cities from 1860 to 1900.

The Negro population has shown a greater increase than the white in each southern city taken separately for the entire period, 1860 to 1900, but together the movement of the white and Negro populations was similar except between 1860 and 1870. That fourteen of the southern cities show an excessive proportional increase of Negro population between 1860 and 1870 is probably due (1) to the very small proportionate Negro population in each of these cities in 1860, the Negroes being almost entirely in the rural districts, and (2) to the exceptional influences following the Civil War which uprooted the rural Negro population that was proportionately larger than the white. The truth of this is corroborated by the per cent of increase by decades for these southern cities taken together. Comparisons with the white population in Northern cities were not made because of the influence of foreign immigration of whites. The per cent of increase of the populations in Southern cities from 1860 to 1870 were white 16.7 per cent, Negro 9o.7 per cent; from 1870 to 1880, white 20.3 per cent, Negro 25.5 per cent; from 1880 to 1890, white 35.7 per cent, Negro 38.7 per cent; from 1890 to 1900, white 20.8 per cent, Negro 20.6 per cent; from 1900 to 1910, white 27.7 per cent, Negro 20.6 per cent. That is, when the proportion between the urban and rural populations of blacks and whites becomes normal, and exceptional influences no longer bear upon the Negro, the two populations show about the same rate of increase in their migrations to these Southern cities. The percent of increase of the Negro population for eight Northern cities (counting all the boroughs of New York City as now constituted as one) was as follows: 1860-1870, 51 per cent; 1870-1880, 36.4 per cent; 1880-1890, 32.3 per cent; 1890-1900, 59.2 per cent. The larger liberty of Northern cities was coupled with the economic call of better wages. And this probably may account for the fact that Southern cities show an increase of whites of 7.7 per cent more than of Negroes between 1900-1910. The migration to both Southern and Northern cities is graphically illustrated in the accompanying diagram.

Diagram I

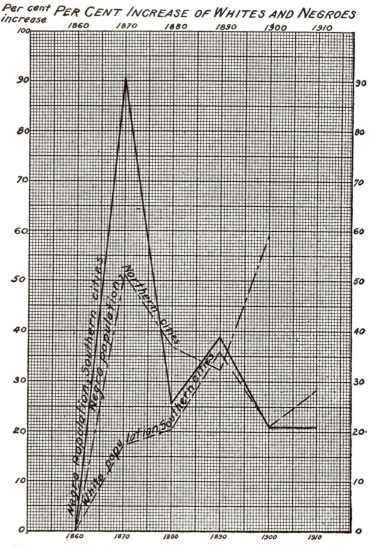

Per cent increase PER CENT INCREASE OF WHITES AND NEGROES

The figures for Southern cities represented in the diagram are given in Table I.

TABLE I. NUMBER AND PER CENT. INCREASE OF WHITE AND NEGRO
POPULATIONS, PRINCIPAL SOUTHERN CITIES, 1860–1900 [1]

	Population 14 cities.		Increase 1860–1870.		Population 15 cities.		Increase 1870–1880.	
	1860.	1870.	No.	Per cent	1870.	1880.	No.	Per cent
White	610,015	712,015	102,000	16.7	715,887	867,403	145,081	20.3
Negro	141,709	270,212	128,503	90.7	272,433	341,907	69,474	25.5

	Population 15 cities.	Increase 1880–1890.		Population 16 cities.	Increase 1890–1900.	
	1890.	No.	Per cent	1900.	No.	Per cent
White	1,183,419	307,542	35.7	1,429,931	246,512	20.8
Negro	485,477	132,316	38.7	585,931	100,054	20.6

	Population 16 cities.	Increase 1900–1910.	
	1910.	No.	Per cent
White	1,817,155	387,224	27.7
Negro	706,352	120,821	20.6

Both the diagram and the table support the conclusion
that the movement of the white and Negro populations to
these cities have been similar under similar conditions and
influences.

[1] Table is based on figures compiled from Eighth Census, *Pop.*, pp. 9, 19, 46,
74, 132, 195, 215, 452, 487, 519; Tenth Census, vol. i, *Pop.*, pp. 416–425;
Eleventh Census, vol. i, *Pop.*, pp. 451–485; Twelfth Census, vol. i, pt. 2, *Pop.*,
pp. cxix–cxxi and *Bulletin 8, Negroes of the United States*, pp. 230–232. For
1860, compare Hoffman, *Race Traits and Tendencies of the American Negro*
p. 10.

In like manner such statistics as are available show that the causes that have concentrated the white population in urban centres have operated likewise to send the Negro thither.

I. The Divorce of the Negro from the Soil.—Witl, other rural populations improvements in agriculture have made fewer workers necessary. In the case of the Negro, the main moving force from the rural districts since 1860 has been the breaking down of the old régime. The decades from 1840 to 1890, except 1870 to 1880, or the period of the " industrial paralysis " after the panic of 1873, were decades of remarkable urban growth in the United States.[1] The first two decades of this time were the years of violent slavery agitation. Then followed the Civil War and the boon of freedom, which gave rise to an unusual mobility of Negro labor. The inevitable *Wanderlust* which sudden social upheaval entails was increased by Ku-Klux terrorism and the breaking down of the slave plantation system.[2] Thousands of the wandering freedmen flocked to the Union army posts which were located in towns and cities.

This was only the beginning. The landless freedman furnished occasion for the creation of the share-tenant and crop-lien systems. In many cases these handicaps often became intolerable under dishonest merchants, unscrupulous landlords, and ill-treatment by overseers.[3] All this tended to loosen the hold of the Negro tenant upon the soil.

Simultaneously with these dominant forces in agriculture, another began to be felt. The one crop of cotton or

---

[1] Weber, *op. cit.*, pp. 24-27, 162.

[2] Coman, *Industrial History of the United States*, Revised edition, (New York, 1910), pp. 308-9.

[3] Kelsey, *The Negro Farmer*, (Chicago, 1903), pp. 5-103; *vide* pp. 24-28. Du Bois, *The Negro Farmer* in *Bulletin 8*, (Twelfth Census), pp. 79-81.

tobacco taxed the land in many sections year after year until it was worn out. In 1899, 70.5 per cent of Negro farmers reported cotton as the principal source of income. Tobacco formed the principal source of income of 16 per cent of Negro farmers in Virginia, of 30.1 per cent in Kentucky and of 18.7 per cent in Maryland.[1] Compared with the growing industrial pursuits, these old agricultural lands no longer offer attractive returns.[2]

Again, where thrift, improvement in agricultural methods and knowledge develop, just as among other farmers, there begins to be a surplus of hands to the cultivator, and Negroes turn toward better paid employment in the urban centres.

It is true that there are large uncultivated, virgin areas of the Southwest, especially in Alabama, Mississippi, Louisiana, Arkansas, and Texas, that are calling loudly for farm labor. The population these areas can support is very considerable and the returns to labor are better than in many of the older agricultural sections. Granting this, the tendency of modern civilization and improvements in facilities for transportation favors the urban centers. So that migration is easier toward the city than away from it or toward these untilled agricultural areas. *The Negro is in the population stream.*

II. The Migration of the Negro to Industrial and Commercial centers.—A study of the growth of the Southern cities shows influences at work similar to those of other sections. Statistics of manufactures of the United States Censuses are not altogether conclusive or reliable, but they measurably indicate conditions. We turn to these records for light upon the Southern situation.

---

[1] DuBois, *op. cit.*, p. 77.

[2] Kelsey, *Some Causes of Negro Emigration: Charities*, New York, vol. xv, no. 1, pp. 15-17; *cf.* DuBois, *op. cit.*, pp. 73-74.

A study of the value of manufactured products of six-teen Southern cities shows that there was a marked increase during the twenty-five years from 1880 to 1905. The in-dustrial centers, Chattanooga, Tennessee, and Birmingham, Alabama, have come into prominence in the decade, 1890-1900, and show an increase in value of products of 17.8 per cent and 78.9 per cent respectively. The comparatively small increase during 1890-1900 for Richmond, Va.; Charleston, S. C.; Augusta and Savannah, Ga., and Mobile, Ala., was probably due to unknown local causes and to a reaction during the industrial crisis of 1892-1894 from the excessive increases of the preceding decade. Yet these cities along with nine of the others show remarkable in-crease in the total value of products for the entire twenty years from 1880 to 1900. Richmond, with an increase of 39 per cent and Savannah, with an increase of 90.3 per cent, were the only cities which had an increase of less than one hundred per cent in value of products during the score of years from 1880 to 1900. The total increase in value of products from 1880 to 1900 for 14 of the cities (Chattanooga and Birmingham being omitted) was 143.3 per cent. The following comparative statement in Table II shows the increase in the value of products of manufactures in sixteen Southern cities from 1880 to 1905, and gives the detailed figures which are the bases of the preceding conclusion. (See p. 21.)

Along with the increase of production has gone the growth in the average number of wage-earners in manufac-turing establishments. Each city made a decided advance in the average number of wage-earners in manufactures during the twenty years from 1880 to 1900. In that period, out of fourteen cities, two increased over 300 per cent in the average number of wage-earners, two cities increased over 240 per cent in the average number of wage-earners,

five cities increased over 100 per cent and the remaining
five cities showed an increase of 76.3 per cent, 57 per cent,
39.8 per cent, 18.8 per cent, and 7.5 per cent respectively
Chattanooga, Tenn., and Birmingham, Ala., from 1890 to

TABLE II. TOTAL VALUE OF PRODUCTS, INCLUDING CUSTOM WORK AND RE-
PAIRING, OF MANUFACTURES IN SIXTEEN SOUTHERN CITIES, 1880–1905 [1]

Cities.	Total value of products.				
	1880.	1890.	1900.	Per cent increase 1880–1900.	1905.[2]
	$	$	$		$
Wilmington	13,205,370	24,568,125	34,053,324	157.9	30,390,039
Baltimore	78,417,304	141,723,599	161,249,240	105.6	151,546,580
Washington [3].....	11,882,316	39,331,437	47,667,622	301.2	18,359,159
Norfolk	1,455,987	5,100,408	9,397,355	545.4	5,900,129
Richmond	20,790,106	27,792,672	28,900,616	39.0	28,202,607
Charleston	2,732,590	9,005,421	9,562,387	249 9	6,007,094
Atlanta	4,861,727	13,074,037	16,707,027	243.6	25,745,650
Augusta	3,139,029	9,244,850	10,041,900	219.9	8,829,305
Savannah	3,396,297	6,319,c66	6,461,816	90.3	6,340,004
Louisville	35,423,203	54,515,226	78,746,390	122.3	83,204,125
Chattanooga......	....	10,216,109	12,033,780	17.8 [4]	15,193,909
Memphis	4,413,422	13,244,538	17,923,058	306.1	21,348,817
Nashville	8,597,278	14,590,823	18,469,823	114.8	23,109,601
Birmingham......	....	7,034,248	12,581,066	78.9 [4]	7,592,958
Mobile	1,335,579	3,826,399	4,451,062	233.3	4,942,331
New Orleans	18,808,096	48,295,449	63,514,505	237.7	84,604,006
Total	208,458,304	427,882,407	531,760,971	143.3 [5]	521,316,314

[1] Compiled from Census Reports: 1880, 10th Census, *Manufactures*, pp.
xxiv, xxv; 1890–1900, 12th Census, vol. viii, *Manufactures, Part ii*, pp. 7, 108,
115, 134, 279, 301, 335, 831, 848, 908; 1905, 12th Census, *Manufactures, Part
ii*, pp. 20, 142, 152, 179, 339, 361, 403, 1025, 1056, 1127.

[2] In Tables ii and iii the figures of Manufactures from 1880 to 1900 are not ex-
actly comparable with those of 1905, because the census of 1905 was limited to
manufacturing establishments and excluded all neighborhood work and establishments for custom work and repairing. Hence percentage of increase was not
worked out for this period.

[3] Figures for Washington, D. C., apply to the District of Columbia and include
governmental establishments.   [4] Increase 1890–1900.

[5] Increase per cent for 14 cities from 1880 to 1900, exclusive of Chattanooga
and Birmingham.

1900 increased 5.2 per cent and 105.6 per cent respectively. Omitting these, the other fourteen cities taken together increased in the number of wage-earners during the twenty years from 1880 to 1900, 60.9 per cent. Table III, which follows, brings into full view this large and constant increase in the average number of wage-earners in manufacturing establishments, exclusive of proprietors, salaried officers, clerks, etc.

TABLE III.   AVERAGE NUMBER OF WAGE-EARNERS [1] ENGAGED IN MANUFACTURES IN SIXTEEN SOUTHERN CITIES, 1880-1905 [2]

	Average Number of Wage-earners.				
	1880.	1890.	1900.	Per cent increase, 1880-1900.	1905.[4]
Wilmington, Del.	7,852	13,370	16,055	104.5	13,554
Baltimore, Md.	56,338	76,489	78,738	39.8	65,224
Washington, D. C.	7,146	20,406	24,693	245.5	17,281
Norfolk, Va.	752	2,391	4,334	476.3	3,063
Richmond, Va.	14,047	16,891	16,692	18.8	12,883
Charleston, S. C.	2,146	4,684	5,027	134.2	3,450
Atlanta, Ga.	3,680	7,957	9,356	154.2	11,891
Augusta, Ga.	4,518	5,714	7,092	57.0	4,839
Savannah, Ga.	1,130	2,419	2,870	154.1	3,330
Louisville, Ky.	17,103	24,159	29,926	7.5	24,985
Chattanooga, Tenn.[3]	......	5,200	5,472	5.2	6,984
Memphis, Tenn.	2,268	5,497	8,433	271.8	8,153
Nashville, Tenn.	4,791	7,275	8,447	76.3	8,435
Birmingham, Ala.[3]	......	3,247	6,675	105.6	3,987
Mobile, Ala.	704	2,719	2,827	301.5	2,496
New Orleans, La.	9,504	22,342	19,435 [5]	104.5	17,631
Total	131,979	212,313	233,925	60.9 [6]	208,186

[1] Does not include proprietors, salaried officers, clerks, etc.

[2] 1880, Tenth Census, *Manufactures*, pp. xxiv, xxv; 1890 and 1900, 11th Census, *Manufactures, Part ii*, pp. 7. 108, 115, 134, 279, 300, 335, 831, 848, 908; 1905, 12th Census, vol. viii, *Manufactures, Part ii*, pp. 20, 142, 152, 179, 339, 361, 403, 1025, 1056, 1127.   [3] No return for 1880.

[4] Figures for 1905 are less and are not comparable with preceding figures, because in 1905 all neighborhood work and establishments for custom work and repairing were excluded.

[5] Does not include cotton compressing in 1900.

[6] Fourteen cities; Chattanooga and Birmingham are omitted.

The industrial pull of Southern cities, then, is shown both by the increase in the average number of wage-earners and in the total value of manufactured products.

There is no reason to doubt that commercial enterprise has operated and kept pace with industrial activity in causing the growth of these urban centers. Figures for the trade of these sixteen Southern cities are not available. However, we have side lights upon the commercial life in the amount of railroad building that has taken place in the South since 1860. In 1860, there were only 8,317 miles of railroad in the thirteen states from Maryland and Delaware to Arkansas and Texas. In 1900, there were 46,-735.86 miles in the same territory, an increase of 461.9 per cent. From 1900 to 1905 this increased to 55,239.22 miles or 18.2 per cent in the five years.[1] Likewise the traffic operations, including total tonnage, and freight, passenger, express and mail earnings of selected groups of railways covering most of this territory, increased very rapidly from 1890 to 1900. In the ten years, from 1890 to 1900, the tonnage increased from 63,597,120 tons to 121,180,317 tons or 90.5 per cent; and total earnings went from $113,616,184.45 in 1890 to $168,606,233 in 1900, an increase of 48.4 per cent in ten years.

As these industrial and commercial forces affect the population, the Negro without doubt shares to a considerable extent the influence. That the Negro has been a large labor factor in the South is a patent fact. All the data available indicate that he has been affected by economic influences similar to those which have moved the white population toward the urban centers.

The most decisive set of facts is the growth in the number of whites and Negroes in gainful occupations in South-

---

[1] *Statistical Abstract of the United States*, 1909, table 143, p. 261.

ern cities. The census returns of 1890 and 1900 for a number of Southern cities were sufficient for an inference. For some occupations figures for 1890 were not available, and in other occupations some cities were not reported in 1890. So a selected list of occupations was taken.

The comparisons of those occupations selected are striking. Among the males, for domestic and personal service occupations, from 1890 to 1900, the white wage-earners increased 42.3 per cent and the Negro wage-earners increased 31.1 per cent. Here we see the influence of the growth of wealthy classes in the industrial and commercial centers, who require increasing numbers to supply their developing wants. In trade and transportation occupations, while the number of white wage-earners increased 25.2 per cent from 1890 to 1900, the Negro wage-earners increased 39.1 per cent during the same decade. For the same period, in manufacturing and mechanical pursuits, the white workers increased 6.1 per cent and the Negro workers increased 12.1 per cent. This indicates the dependence of the growing industry of the South upon its black male workers and shows how strong upon them is the economic pull.

For the females, the increases are no less telling, especially for Negro workers. In ten selected occupations for Southern cities, the white female workers decreased 29.1 per cent and the Negro female workers increased 36 per cent from 1890 to 1900. The decrease for the whites was due to an excessive decrease among dressmakers, milliners and seamstresses, which may be a discrepancy of the census returns.

The full list of selected occupations in Southern cities for 1890 and 1900 are given in full in Table IV, following:

TABLE IV. INCREASE OF WHITE AND NEGRO WAGE-EARNERS IN SELECTED OCCUPATIONS, SOUTHERN CITIES, 1890–1900 [1]

Occupation.	No. of cities.	Male. Native white. 1890.	1900.	Per cent increase.	Negro. 1890.	1900.	Per cent increase.
Domestic and personal service..	..	29,407	41,854	42.3	54,179	71,047	31.1
Barbers, hairdressers........	10	1,436	2,208	....	1,946	2,317	.....
Bartenders	8	1,688	2,486	....	277	389	.....
Laborers (not specified)	10	19,843	27,759	.....	35,868	51,346	.....
Restaurant and saloon keepers	9	1,577	2,107	.....	377	474	....
Servants and waiters	10	1,395	1,128	.....	15,358	16,071	.....
Watchmen, policemen, detectives, etc................	10	3,441	6,166	.....	353	450	.....
Trade and transportation......	..	71,291	89,294	25.2	18,305	25,459	39.1
Agents, collectors and commercial travelers	10	8,571	13,031	.....	287	411	.....
Bankers, brokers and officials (bank)	8	2,309	1,824	.....	76	13	.....
Draymen, hackmen, teamsters [2]	10	6,385	8,117	.....	11,246	14,545	.....
Messengers, packers, porters, etc...................	9	3.302	4,486	.....	3,554	6,225	.....
Steam railway employees	10	11,033	11,532	...	2,213	3,048	.....
Street railway employees	8	1,987	3,366	.....	85	170	.....
Bookkeepers, accountants, etc. [3]	10	37,704	46,638	.....	844	1,057	.....
Manufacturing and mechanical pursuits	..	55,236	64,288	16.3	11,548	12,887	11.6
Bakers and butchers........	9	4,111	4,512	.....	632	640	.....
Blacksmiths .... [4]	10	3,722	4,003	.....	852	935	.....
Boot and shoemakers and repairers	10	2,195	1,816	.....	1,184	965	.....
Carpenters and joiners	10	12,947	12,394	.....	3,029	2,762	.....
Cotton and textile mill operatives...................	7	2,648	2,534	.....	258	281	.....
Engineers, firemen (not locomotive)	10	3,379	5,151	.....	881	1,224	.....
Iron and steel workers	9	3,366	4,808	.....	779	752	.....
Machinists	10	5,086	8,088	.....	92	174	.....
Marble and stone cutters	5	1,009	906	.....	150	149	.....
Masons (brick and stone)....	6	2,663	2,362	.....	731	1,264	.....
Painters, glaziers, varnishers..	10	6,807	7,372	.....	875	782	.....
Plasterers	7	672	633	.....	886	811	.....
Plumbers, gas and steam fitters	7	1,925	2,646	.....	113	151	.....
Saw and planing mill employees...................	7	2,543	4,409	.....	749	1,062	.....
Tailors...................	10	2,163	2,654	.....	337	307	.....
Total	..	155,934	195,436	25.3	84,032	109,393	30.2

TABLE IV.—*Concluded.*

Occupation.	No. of cities.	Female.					
		Native white.			Negro.		
		1890.	1900.	Per cent increase.	1890.	1900.	Per cent increase.
Housekeepers and stewardesses.	10	1,475	1,956	.....	752	513	.....
Laborers (not specified).......	10	332	712	.....	676	901	.....
Laundresses	10	1,543	2,409	.....	25,968	41,386	.....
Nurses and midwives..........	10	781	2,472	.....	1,097	3,691	.....
⁵ Servants	10	10,176	9,983	.....	47,198	56,729	.....
Saleswomen	7	2,633	4,808	.....	37	28	.....
Dressmakers, milliners, seamstresses	10	41,313	22,007	.....	6,528	6,859	.....
Tailoresses	6	2,814	2,950	.....	164	131	.....
Total	..	61,067	47,297 ⁶	29.1 ⁶	81,027	110,238	36.0

The evidence, then, that the economic call of Southern cities has received response from Negroes as from whites is fairly conclusive. That the economic motive of the Negro has had a large place in causing his migration to urban centers is further shown by the testimony of Negro wage-earners in a Northern city.

In a personal canvass in New York City, 365 wage-earners were asked their reasons for coming to New York

NOTES FOR TABLE IV.

[1] Figures for 1890 from Eleventh Census, *Pop.*, *Part ii*, pp. 630-703; for 1900, Twelfth Census, *Occupations*, Table 43. The cities are from the list in Tables III and IV *supra*.

[2] Includes office-boys, shippers, and helpers in stores in 1900, probably not separated in 1890.   [3] Includes clerks and copyists.

[4] Includes some wheelwrights for all cities except one.

[5] Includes waitresses in 1900.   [6] Decrease.

City. In reply to the question put in this direct manner
210 out of the total 365 wage-earners gave replies; of these,
99 or 47.1 per cent gave answers that are easily classified
as economic. The other replies have been grouped under
" family " reasons, 68 or 32.4 per cent, and " individual "
reasons, 43 or 20.5 per cent. Many cases in the last two
groupings, as appear below (pp. 31-32), would probably be
seen to have an underlying economic cause, if we knew
more of their history. The 99 answers classed as economic
were as follows:

TABLE V. ECONOMIC REASONS GIVEN BY 99 WAGE-EARNERS FOR COMING
TO NEW YORK CITY, 1909.

To " get work " or " find work "	38
To secure " better wages " or " more money "	19
With former employers	18
To complete trade training	2
To engage in work previously assured	4
To " better my condition "	15
" Business low at home "	1
" Wanted to buy house at home by (with) money made here "	1
" Seeking business "	1
Total	99

This evidence is further corroborated by a record of the
wages of 64 of the 365 wage-earners before and after their
coming to New York City. For 38 males and 26 females
statements of the wages received just previously to their
coming to New York City and of their present wages were
secured. These figures are presented because they suggest
that a wider survey of such facts would probably be in line
with the body of data given above. For instance, of 37
men, the median weekly wage before their coming to New
York City was in the wage-group $6.00 to $6.99, and after
coming, the median weekly wage increased so that it was
in the wage-group $10.00 to $10.99. Of the 26 women,
the median weekly wage was in the wage-group $4.00 to

$4.99 before their coming to New York City and advanced so that it was in the group $6.00 to $6.99 after coming. These facts indicate a decided response to the higher wage attraction of New York City. It should be remarked that the wage-earner in his migration to secure higher wages seldom takes into consideration the higher cost of living in New York City. Table VI, following, gives the details of the comparison:

TABLE VI. WEEKLY WAGES RECEIVED BY 64 INDIVIDUALS BEFORE AND AFTER COMING TO NEW YORK CITY, 1909.

Wages.	Males.		Females.	
	Before.	After.	Before.	After.
Less than $3.00	..	..	9	..
$3.00–$3.99	8	..	3	3
$4.00–$4.99	3	..	3	3
$5.00–$5.99	6	3	6	3
$6.00–$6.99	6	3	1	7
$7.00–$7.99	1	8	2	6
$8.00–$8.99	4	..	..	2
$9.00–$9.99	.	4	2	2
$10.00–$10.99	3	5	..	..
$11.00–$11.99	1	4	..	..
$12.00–$12.99	1	2	..	..
$13.00 and over	4	9[1]	..	..
Total	37	38	26	26

In the economic movement to the Northern cities, the activity of employment agencies (especially for female domestic help) with drummers and agents in Southern communities has served to spread tales of high wages and to provide transportation for large numbers.[2] Again, many who have been to the urban centers return for visits to

[1] One individual replied " less than now in New York City."

[2] Kellor, Out of Work, pp. 73, 83.

their more rural home communities with show of better wages in dress, in cash and in conversation.[1]

The conclusion of the matter, therefore, is that the Negro is responding to the call of commerce and industry and is coming to the urban centers under economic influences similar to those that move his fellows.

III. Secondary or Individual Causes of the Negro's Movement Cityward.—It requires only a brief survey of the legislation in several of the Southern states to understand that this has played a part in uprooting the population from the soil and transplanting it in the urban centers.

The trend of legislation everywhere has been to make the city attractive at the expense of the rural districts. First among these measures have been the improved educational facilities provided by municipal authorities. In the South, this has come since 1865. Parks and recreation centers are rapidly being added. General regulation of rights and privileges has been made with the city in the foreground, and many another measure has favored the urban centers.

Labor legislation in the South that affects the Negro population has been of two kinds, aside from the laws to regulate or prohibit the exodus of laborers through the activity of labor agents or runners:[2] (1) that applying to

---

[1] *Cf.* Tucker, *Negro Craftsmen in New York*, in *Southern Workman*, September, 1907, p. 550.

[2] For statute provisions of state governments, see *Twenty-second Annual Report of the Commissioner of Labor, Labor Laws of the United States*, pp. 129, sec. 4165; 133-135, secs. 6345-6856; 146-147, secs. 3695-3696, 3905, 4057; 153, secs. 5357-58, 5383; 155-56; acts of 1901, no. 101, secs. 1-3; acts of 1905, no. 49, secs. 1-3; 157-59, act no. 219, sec. 1; act no. 225, secs. 7-18; 278, secs. 2530, 2641-42; 281, sec. 3233-34; 291, sec. 4732; 495-501, secs. 1350, 2722-2739A; 706, sec. 2139; 1228-29, secs. 2717-2720; 1231-32, secs. 338, 358; 1251-52, secs. 3794, 4339-42; 1339-40, sec. 3657D. *Vide* also, *Digest and Summaries of Certain*

the industrial centers and serving to make conditions of labor on railroads, in mines, and other places where Negroes are employed more attractive and payment of wages more certain and frequent than in the case of labor upon the farm and plantation; (2) that dealing with the relations of landlord and tenant which in practical operation often makes the life of the tenant and farm-hand very hard. Coupled with the ignorance of the usual Negro peasant, these laws are sometimes tools of coercion.[1]

Another line of secondary or individual causes is shown in the reasons for coming to New York City given by wage-earners mentioned above (p. 27). The tabulation of answers indicates that the influences drawing individuals to New York City are, on the one hand, family relationships. These cases, 68 or 32.4 per cent of the 210 replies noted above, have been classified as those who came because of parents, because of husband or wife, or because of other relatives. On the other hand, there are the individual inclinations. The latter, 43 or 20.5 per cent of the 210 re-

Classes of Laws Affecting Labor,—Mechanics' Liens, pp. 37-38, 43, 44, 49, 50, 55, 61-62, 70-72, 74.

[1] The laws referred to are framed in terms of the regulation of contracts of employment, violation of contract, and contracts of employment with intent to defraud. Breach of contract in either set of cases is usually a misdemeanor (criminal act instead of a civil tort) with a penalty of fines (or imprisonment in Florida). Often in practical operation, they place the tenant and farm laborer at the discretion or mercy of the landlord. The writer has made repeated visits to many rural communities in Ala., Ga., Fla., Miss., and La., and has observed how these legislative measures serve as barriers to thrift among the landless Negro farmers. A number of the youths have expressed their conviction that since their fathers and mothers have accumulated nothing after years of labor on the land, they do not intend to stay on the plantation to repeat the process. For provisions of statutes: See Commissioner of Labor, *op. cit.*, pp. 133-34, secs. 6845-46; 147, sec. 5030; 284, chaps. 703-704, secs. 1146-1148.

plies, are grouped under restlessness, attraction of New York City, unattractiveness of former residence, and miscellaneous. These groupings and designations are given as suggestive only to facilitate the understanding of the mental attitude of the Negro wage-earner. Their more or less economic tinge may be seen. The reasons classified as " family " and as " individual " are reported in detail in Table VII, following:

TABLE VII. REASONS GIVEN IN 1909 BY WAGE-EARNERS SHOWING WHY THEY CAME TO NEW YORK CITY, 1909.

Family reasons (68 or 32.4 per cent. of 210).			
On account of parents.	On account of husband or wife.	On account of other relatives.	Total.
" Brought here by parents " 12	" Relatives of wife here " 1	" A son here " 2	
" With mother " 6	" Wife here " 1	" To visit a brother and remained ".... 5	
" Came with mother who was here ".... 4	" To follow husband " . 1	" Had a sister here ". 9	
" Father was here ".. 2	" Came with husband " 7	" My health was bad and came to live with sister " 1	
" On account of death of father "........ ... 1	" My husband was working on a ship coming here "...... 1	To live with other relatives on account of death of mother 4	
" Father transferred in revenue service " 1		Through influence of other relatives . 10	
Total 26	Total 11	Total 31	68

TABLE VII—*Concluded.*

Individual reasons (43 or 20.5 per cent of 210).			
Restlessness.—16	Attraction of New York City.—15	Former residence, unattractive.—6	Total—43.

Restlessness.—16	Attraction of New York City.—15	Former residence, unattractive.—6
" Thought I would like the place as a change;" wanted " to be going somewhere."	" I wanted to come out this way."	" To say I was leaving home like everybody else." (From St. Martin's Island.)
" Was in Rhode Island and wanted a change."	" Wanted to come to a larger (place); to travel to see the world."	" Got tired of Boston and came to New York."
" Thought I'd like to make a change."	" Passing through several summers; stopped."	" Got tired of Virginia; came to visit friend; remained."
" Wanted to make a change."	" Came out with friends who were coming; been back and forth."	" Got tired of Baltimore; thought I'd see some of New York."
" To change cities and see New York."	" Was running on the boat to New York and stopped for a while."	" Got tired of home, that's all."
" Thought I would like change; to be going somewhere."	" Just to see New York; was traveling and stopped."	" To get away from home for a change."
" Just for a change."		Miscellaneous.—6
" Just for a change."	" Took a notion to come; wanted to come North."	
" Thought I'd make a change; came North to try it."	" Liked New York after seeing it as a sailor in the Navy."	" Came to get married."
" Just to be coming." (To New York)	" Thought I would like New York."	" Stopped on way to Boston, robbed in Jersey City."
" For recreation; to change cities."	" Thought I'd like New York."	" Came to America to go to school." (From S. Hampton, Bermuda.)
" Traveling and stopped."	" Wanted to see the place."	" To learn architecture."
" Split the difference of time."	" To see the place and be with sister."	" To visit friends; got married."
" Felt like traveling."	" To see the city; friend wrote me of sights of the great city."	" To see and learn and improve my ability."
" Had a roaming mind —came here from Chicago."	" Heard talk of enjoyable life here."	
" Felt like traveling."	" Came here from Cincinnati; had read a great deal of New York City and wanted to see it."	

Another individual cause operates especially upon the more able and intelligent classes and sends them to Northern cities. The restriction by " Jim Crow " legislation and by custom of the rights and privileges of persons of color in Southern communities leads some of them to migrate North. They long for a larger liberty for themselves and particularly for their children, which the hard conditions of Southern communities do not give. They come North to gain this and to escape the proscriptions.[1] They settle in the cities. A similar force probably operates in a few sections of the South to send Negro families to the security of the urban centers.[2]

The final conclusion from these facts concerning the causes operating upon the Negro population has been clearly indicated in the above discussion. Such fundamental economic and social causes do not cease to operate suddenly. So far as the development of the South is concerned, the agricultural, industrial and commercial movement is in its infancy, and it will doubtless be of an indefinite growth. The secondary and individual causes will continue to play their part. The Negro will be affected in a manner similar to that of the Southern white population. Any rural improvement or " back-to-the-land " movement should recognize that along with the whites, Negroes will continue to migrate to the urban centers and that they will come to the cities in comparatively large numbers to stay. The problem alike of statesman, race leader, and philanthropist is to understand the conditions of segregation and oppositions due to race prejudices that are arising as a sequel to this urban concentration and to co-operate with the Negro in his effort to learn to live in the city as well as the country.

[1] *Economic Analysis of American Prejudice*, by Dr. Wm. L. Bulkley, in *The Colored American Magazine*, July, 1909, pp. 17, 19, 20-21.

[2] *Cf. Darkest America*, by Kelly Miller in *New England Magazine*, April, 1904.

Although it requires serious attention, the situation is a hopeful one. Improvement in the living and working conditions has its effect upon the health and morals of Negroes just as it has in the case of other elements of the population. Intelligence is essentially a matter of education and training. Good housing, pure milk and water supply, sufficient food and clothing, which adequate wages allow, street and sewer sanitation, have their direct effect upon health and physique. And municipal protection and freedom from the pressure of the less moral elements of the environing group go a long way toward elevating standards of morality. In spite of the limits which the neglect and prejudice of a white public sets to opportunities for improvement, Negroes do show progress along these lines.

Speaking first of the health of Negroes in cities, an index is given in the general death-rate.[1] In the period from 1871 to 1904, the death rate for the white and Negro populations of several Southern cities is summarized by Mr. Hoffman.[2] Of the consolidated death-rate of the white population, he says,

For only two cities are the returns complete for the entire period of thirty-four years. The tendency of the rate has been *persistently downward* from 26.7 per 1,000 in 1871 to 20.6 in 1886 and 17.4 in 1904. Commencing with the rate for the year 1871, the general death-rate of the white popula-

[1] *Vide* Hoffman, *The General Death Rate of Large American Cities, 1871-1904*, in *Quarterly Publications of the American Statistical Association*, new series, vol. x, no. 73, March, 1906. Mr. Hoffman says: " While the general death-rate is of very limited value for the purpose of comparison in the case of different localities, it is, I am satisfied, after a very careful investigation and much experience, of quite considerable value in making local comparison of the present health conditions with the past."

[2] *Op. cit.*, pp. 5-8. The cities are Baltimore, 1871-1904; New Orleans, 1871-1904; District of Columbia, 1876-1904; Louisville, Ky., 1890-1904; Memphis, Tenn., 1876-1904.

tion of Southern cities shows an *upward direction* at different times *during twelve years,* and a *downward* direction *during twenty-one years,* following in this respect practically the same course as the corresponding death-rate for Northern and Western cities combined. The year of *maximum mortality* was *1878*, due to a yellow fever epidemic, while the year of *minimum mortality* was, as in the case of the Northern and Western cities, *1903.*

In reference to the table for the Negro population he says,[1]

Without exception, the death-rates are materially in excess of the corresponding death-rates of the white population, but there has also been in this case *a persistent decline* in the general death-rate from 38.1 per 1,000 in 1871 to 32.9 in 1886 and 28.1 in 1904. Commencing with the rate for the year 1871, the general death-rate of the colored population of Southern cities at different times assumed an *upward* direction *during fifteen years* and a *downward* direction *during eighteen years*, departing in this respect from the corresponding mortality of the white population of Southern cities and the general population of Northern and Western cities, the tendency of which was more distinctly towards a definite improvement. The year of *maximum mortality* for the colored population was *1873*, while the year of *minimum mortality* was *1903.*

The general correspondence and few divergencies of the two death-rates are more clearly seen from the following diagram,[2] adapted from Hoffman's study already cited:

[1] *Op. cit.,* pp. 7-8. (Italics are mine.)

[2] In the *Biennial Report of the Board of Health of New Orleans, La., 1906-1907,* this diagram of Mr. Hoffman is reproduced with the following comment: (p. 113) "The colored mortality has not only been excessive, but has borne no relation whatever to the white mortality curve, being on the ascending scale at times when the white mortality was clearly on the decrease." A comparison with Mr. Hoffman's words about the two death-rates quoted above and a glance at the curves supply sufficient commentary upon this biased view.

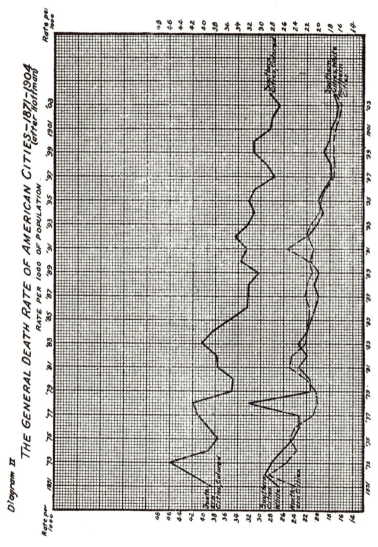

Diagram II — THE GENERAL DEATH RATE OF AMERICAN CITIES—1871-1904 (after Hoffman)

Other data[1] for two of the cities investigated by Mr.

[1] *Mortality Among Negroes in Cities*, Atlanta University Pubs., no. 1, (Atlanta, Ga., 1896), p. 51; *vide* pp. 21-25; and 2nd ed., 1903, pp. 11-15.

Hoffman, and for three other cities (Atlanta, Ga., Charleston, S. C., and Richmond, Va.) from 1882 to 1905 furnish results similar to his and indicate likewise that while the general death-rate for the Negro population is uniformly in excess of that of the white, *there is a tendency downward*. For example, in Atlanta, Ga., the death-rates from 1882 to 1885 were for the white population, 18.22 per 1,000, Negro, 37.96; from 1886 to 1890, white, 19.25, Negro, 33.41; from 1891 to 1905, white, 18.03 per 1,000, Negro, 32.76. Baltimore, Md., Charleston, S. C., Memphis, Tenn., and Richmond, Va., show a similar decrease, except that the white and Negro populations of Baltimore show an increase in the third period, 1891 to 1905, and the rate of the Negro population of Charleston increased in the second period, 1886 to 1890.

We see, then, that while the death-rate of Negroes in Southern cities has been considerably in excess of that of the whites, there has been at the same time a similar tendency toward improvement.

And where there is unprejudiced effort the death-rate among Negroes is affected favorably by improved living conditions. The chief health-officer of Richmond, Va., Dr. E. C. Levy, has sounded a note which is not mere prophecy.[1] He said, in 1906, " There is no doubt whatsoever but that the introduction of better sanitation among the colored people would have great influence on their high death-rate, but whether, after all, it can be brought down as low as the white rate, is a matter which can not be foretold." Again, in 1907, he says,

We must clearly face the issue that the first fruits of improved sanitation in Richmond will most probably be seen in a lower-

[1] *Annual Reports of the Health Department of the City of Richmond, Va.*, 1906, p. 22; 1907, p. 34; 1908, pp. 39-40.

ing of the death-rate among the colored people, as conditions among them are so much worse at present, but this in turn will gradually react on the white race.

And, in 1908, this significant paragraph occurs in his report:

The white death-rate in Richmond during 1908 was 17.48 per 1000; the colored rate was 29.21 per 1000. Although the colored rate was thus 67 per cent higher than the white rate, the decrease in the colored rate from 1907 was greater than the decrease in the white rate, the 1907 rates being 18.11 for whites and 32.99 for Negroes.

Out of a total decrease of 166 in the number of deaths in 1908 compared with 1907, the white decrease was 27, while the colored decrease was 139. From the time that I entered office I have predicted that improved sanitation would benefit the Colored race more quickly than the white, and the figures above given justify this conclusion.

The statement of this health officer points to experience rather than to prejudiced notions about the physical weaknesses of Negroes.

From both the statistician and the sanitarian, therefore, comes the word that while the health of Negroes in cities is worse than that of whites, it shows a tendency to improve similar to that of the white population when a fairly impartial treatment is accorded.

As with health, so with other phases of the Negro's city life. There is no place for pessimism. Improvements in intelligence and in moral conditions can not be counted by case and set down in figures and tables.[1] But any one at all familiar either by reading or recollection with the

[1] *Cf.* Ray Stannard Baker, in *American Magazine*, Feb. and March, 1908, and *Following the Color Line*, (New York, 1909), pp. 54-55.

condition of the Negro at the beginning of his freedom,
who now takes an impartial and unprejudiced view of his
intellectual and social life in urban communities, will come
to no other conclusion than that in the face of peculiar
whims and prejudices a large and increasing number in
the group is arising to the full consciousness of a freeman
and has assimilated the best that America affords in morals
and intelligence; and that they are vitally concerned for
the uplift of themselves and their people, persistently seeking to partake of all that makes for progress.[1]

For the whole Negro population in cities some light is
thrown upon developments by the few facts at hand on
crime among Negroes.[2] Statistics of crime are, of course,
of limited worth in judging of moral conditions.   Arrests
and prison commitments have many factors which figures
do not show and are quite as much a commentary upon the
white communities at large as upon the unfortunate Negro
law-breakers.   Yet, along with other facts, these records
of crime are a part of the social barometer.

An analysis of three periods of crime (prior to 1866-
1867; 1867 to 1880, and 1880 to 1903) made by Mr.
Monroe N. Work gives indicative results.   Speaking of

---

[1] For a large body of facts and opinions on this point see *Atlanta
University Pubs., no. 8*, pp. 64-79; 108-110; 154-190. Personal observation during residence of the past twelve years in Louisville, Ky.,
Memphis and Nashville, Tenn., Atlanta, Ga., Chicago, and New York,
and during visits to Baltimore, Md., Washington, D. C., Norfolk and
Richmond, Va., Savannah and Augusta, Ga., Chattanooga, Tenn.,
Birmingham and Mobile, Ala., New Orleans, La., and smaller cities
has afforded the author of this essay considerable opportunity to
know at first-hand this phase of Negro city life.

[2] *Atlanta University Pubs., no. 9, Notes on Negro Crime: Crime in
Cities*, by M. N. Work (Atlanta, Ga., 1904), pp. 18-32; *cf*. pp. 49-54.
Vide also Kellor, *Experimental Sociology*, pp. 250 ff.

arrests per thousand of the Negro population in nine cities, he says,[1]

Taking the period from 1866 to 1882, it appears that at some time during this period the arrest-rate, with the possible exception of St. Louis, for each of the cities decreased. From 1882 to 1892-1896 there was, with some exceptions, a marked increase in the arrest-rates of the several cities. This was especially true of Chicago, Cincinnati, Washington and St. Louis. From 1892-1896 to 1902-1903 there appears to have been a general tendency for the Negro arrest-rates of these cities to decrease. It appears that, on the whole, we are warranted in concluding that for the nine cities considered, the rate of Negro arrests per thousand of the Negro population is decreasing.

The rates of jail commitments for Baltimore, Charleston, and St. Louis have increased slowly since the seventies until the nineties, and now apparently are beginning to decrease slightly.

The workhouse commitments for Philadelphia, Washington, Cincinnati, Louisville, Chicago and St. Louis " show a similar tendency to decrease." Penitentiary commitments [2] for Baltimore and Chicago show, on the whole, a decreasing trend. " The rate of annual commitments to the state penitentiary of Illinois from the city of Chicago in 1873 was 4.4; in 1902 the rate was 1.6," the highest rate being in 1873. Mr. Work continues,

The rate of annual commitments to the penitentiary from Baltimore in 1888 was 1.1; in 1902 the rate of annual penitentiary commitments from this city was 1.3; the highest rate of annual penitentiary commitments from Baltimore was 2.0 in 1899. Since 1898-1899 there has been a decrease in the

[1] *Op. cit.*, p. 22.   [2] *Ibid.*, pp. 26-29 *passim.*

annual Negro penitentiary commitments for both cities. The rate per thousand of the Negro population for the number of prisoners received in the Kansas penitentiary was available for four years, as follows: in 1889 and 1890 the rate of annual Negro commitments to the Kansas penitentiary was 1.5; in 1891 and 1892 the rate was 1.3. The rate per thousand of the Negro population for the number of prisoners received annually in the Indiana penitentiary was available for three years, as follows: in 1900 the rate was 2.1; in 1901 the rate was 2.5; and in 1902 the rate was 2.0.

Mr. Work remarks finally,[1]

Summarizing our results, it is seen that police arrests, jail, workhouse and penitentiary commitments appear to have increased during the period from 1890 to 1892-1896. The highest rates of arrests and commitments were about 1893. Since 1894-1896 the tendency of both arrests and commitments to decrease has been notable. The crime-rate for murder is also probably decreasing. It appears, therefore, that the conclusion that crime is probably decreasing among the Negroes of the United States is warranted. The crime-rate of Negroes, North and South, appears at present to be about the same, although the rate of police arrests for some Southern cities is higher than that for the Northern cities. The claim that there is greater criminality among the Negroes of the North than those of the South is probably not true. The fallacy on which this claim was based was in comparing the criminal rate of the Negroes of the North, who live almost entirely in cities, with the criminal rate of the Negroes of the entire South, the great majority of whom live in rural communities.

Besides, differences in age-grouping are usually ignored.

On the whole, therefore, there is firm ground for hope as the Negro becomes adjusted to the urban environment.

---

[1] *Op. cit.*, p. 32.

Since, then, these economic and social causes bid fair to continue their influence for an indefinite time, the concentration of Negroes in urban centers makes imperative the need of knowledge and methods of dealing with the problems that face the Negro and the Nation in these growing urban centers.[1] These questions of how to live in the city are problems of health, of intelligence and of morals. They are economic, social, political, educational and religious. The present essay is an attempt to study carefully the economic problems arising out of the Negro's adjustment in his struggles to make a living and to live in the city as seen in the commercial Metropolis of America; to find out at what he is employed there; to inquire of his efficiency and success, and of the attitude of employer and fellow employee. As we find Negroes rising from the plane of the employed to that of the employer, these questions arise: How does he get into business and what lines does he enter? With what success does he meet? What resourcefulness does he show? What are the reasons for his failures? We want to know what are his relations with the business world with which he deals and the consuming public to whom he caters. These and many other things can be ascertained only by painstaking investigation.

This study aims to be a small contribution to the end that efforts for betterment of urban conditions may be founded upon facts. The material has been treated in two parts— that relating to wage-earners and to business undertakings. In the former the United States Census reports, a personal canvass, and the unpublished schedules for 2,500 families of the New York State Census of 1905, were used as

---

[1] Philadelphia is the only city which has had adequate study. *Vide* DuBois, W. E. B., *The Philadelphia Negro,* (Philadelphia, 1889) and Wright, R. R., Jr., *The Negro in Pennsylvania, a Study in Economic History* (Philadelphia, 1912).

sources; for the latter a block to block canvass was made and records of the business enterprises were secured by personal interviews.

FOOT-NOTE ON THE MANNER AND CAUSES OF CITY CONCEN-TRATION OF POPULATION [1]

The manner of growth has been two-fold: (1) By natural increase through the lowering of the death-rate due partially to improved housing conditions, progress in personal hygiene of the poorer classes and in city sanitation and inspection; (2) by migration: that is, short distance movements by progressive stages from the more rural districts toward the larger centers.[2] In the case of the great cities this may mean increase in density of the most populated areas.[3]

The causes of concentration in cities are the following:

I. The Divorce of Men from the Soil.[4] The diminishing relative importance of elementary wants, improvements in scientific cultivation and in agricultural machinery, and the opening of distant and virgin fields by better transportation have reduced the relative number of workers needed on the soil.

II. The Growth of Commercial Centers.[5] This went hand in hand with the Agrarian Revolution. Trade has been the basis of city founding. The prevailing influence in determining location has been "*a break in transportation.*" Where goods are transferred and where, in addi-

---

[1] *Vide* Weber, *op. cit., passim.*

[2] *Ibid.,* 232 ff.; 241 ff.; 283 ff.; 346-364, *passim.*

[3] A suggestive study on this phase of the city problem has been published recently: *Industrial Causes of Congestion of Population in New York City,* by E. E. Pratt, Ph. D., (New York, 1911), pp. 5-262.

[4] Weber, *op. cit.,* pp. 161-169; 223.

[5] *Ibid.,* pp. 171-173; 181-182; 223-224.

tion, ownership changes hands, urban centers grow up. Wealthy classes arise which require others to supply their increasing and varied wants.

III. The Growth of Industrial Centers.[1] The passage of industry from the household, handicrafts and domestic systems to that of the factory, with the invention of power machinery and modern methods of transportation and communication, draws population away from the rural districts to the industrial centers.

IV. Secondary or Individual Causes.[2] (a) The shifting demand for transfer of labor from agricultural to industrial production was met by the economic motive of workers. (b) Political action has influenced city growth; legislation affecting trade and the migration of labor; centralization of governmental machinery in the cities; legal forms of land tenure, etc. (c) Social advantages such as better education, varied amusements, higher standard of living, intellectual associations and pursuits, draw people to urban centers, while desire for the contact of the moving crowds, for the excitement and apparent ease of city life, serve to make the rural districts distasteful.

[1] Weber, *op. cit.*, pp. 184-191.
[2] *Ibid.*, pp. 210, 213-222.

CHAPTER II

THE NEGRO POPULATION OF NEW YORK CITY

THE Negro population of New York City has had a history similar to that of other Northern cities. Beginning with a small body of slaves, it has since had its problems growing out of the presence of an increasing number of Negroes in the midst of the environing white group. In 1629, The Dutch West India Company pledged itself to furnish slaves to the Colonists of New Amsterdam.[1] A similar resolution was passed by the colony council in 1648 [2] and by 1664 slavery had become of sufficient importance to receive legislative regulation in the Duke of York Code.[3] Both by further importations and by natural increase the Negro population grew until in 1704 it numbered about 1,500; in 1741 it was estimated at about 2,000, and in 1757 about 3,000. Beginning with the first Federal Census of 1790 there was an increase shown by each census except those of 1820 for Brooklyn and of 1850 and 1860 for other parts of New York City, mainly Manhattan.

The figures show a striking contrast in growth between Brooklyn and the other parts of New York City as now constituted, exclusive of Brooklyn. The former had a comparatively small Negro population until after 1860,

[1] *New York Colonial Doc.*, i, 553.

[2] O'Callaghan, *Laws and Ordinances of New Netherlands*, 1637-1674, p. 81.

[3] DuBois, *Some Notes on Negroes of New York City*, p. 5.

but from 1790 the Negro population although small increased steadily, except the one decade between 1810 and 1820. This was a decrease of only 92 or 4.9 per cent of a population less than 2,000. Only one increase, from 1800 to 1810, was less than 13 per cent. Beginning with 5,915 at the Federal census of 1790, the Negro population of the other parts of New York City has shown a high per cent of increase in numbers, above 15 per cent, at eight of the twelve succeeding censuses, and 8.1 per cent and 5.5 per cent at two others. The decreases from 1840 to 1850, 13.2 per cent, and from 1850 to 1860, 7.5 per cent, were probably due to the unfavorable sentiment against the Negroes which arose during the abolition agitation of these periods and which had its effect on the Negro's movements to and from the city. The small increase from 1860 to 1870, 5.5 per cent, was very probably the result of the same causes—of the Civil War disturbances and the New York Draft riots, which deterred Negroes from coming to New York City and sent many Negro residents away.[1] The figures for Manhattan show a similar trend at each census. However, except the periods noted above, there has been a general trend toward increase in both Manhattan and Brooklyn. The Negro population has become a smaller and smaller part of the total population from decade to decade since 1810, but this is because the several streams of foreign immigrants have been large and not because the increase of the Negro population has been small.

Table VIII, which follows, shows the growth of the total and the Negro populations, and brings the full figures to view:

[1] The writer has testimony of contemporary witnesses of these disturbances.

TABLE VIII.—TOTAL AND NEGRO POPULATION OF NEW YORK CITY, AS AT
PRESENT CONSTITUTED, 1704–1910 [1]

Year.	New York City, exclusive of Brooklyn.				Brooklyn.			
	Population.		Increase of Negro population.		Population.		Increase of Negro population.	
	Total.	Negro.	Number.	Per cent	Total.	Negro.[2]	Number.	Per cent
1704 ..	.....	1,500	....	..	......	....	....	..
1741 ..	......	2,000	500	33.3	......	....	....	..
1757 ..	......	3,000	1,000	50.0	......	...	....	..
1790 ..	44,906	5,915	2,915	97.2	4,495	1,478	....	..
1800 ..	73,476	8,626	2,711	45.9	5,740	1,811	333	25.5
1810 ..	111,431	12,116	3,490	40.4	8,303	1,853	42	2.3
1820 ..	140,869	13,100	984	8.1	11,187	1,761	92	4.9[3]
1830 ..	221,743	16,082	2,982	22.8	20,535	2,007	246	13.9
1840 ..	343,501	18,595	2,573	15.6	47,613	2,846	839	41.8
1850 ..	557,233	16,131	2,464	13.2[3]	138,882	4,065	1,219	42.8
1860 ..	895,657	14,927	1,204	7.5[3]	279,122	4,999	934	22.9
1870 ..	1,058,182	15,755	828	5.5	419,921	5,653	654	13.1
1880 ..	1,312,203	22,496	6,741	42.8	599,495	9,153	3,500	61.9
1890 ..	1,668,867	26,330	3,834	17.0	838,547	11,307	2,154	23.5
1900 ..	2,270,620	42,299	15,969	60.6	1,166,582	18,367	7,060	62.5
1910 ..	3,132,532	69,700	27,403	64.8	1,634,351	22,702	4,335	23.6

[1] Figures 1704–1757 from Du Bois, *Notes*, etc., p. 1.

[2] Negro not reported separately 1790 to 1850; includes " slaves " and all other " Free Colored " which does not involve serious error in the earlier censuses.

Census figures 1790–1910 are from the latest revisions of the Bureau of the Census. Figures for same area, outside of Manhattan and Brooklyn, are estimates of censuses 1790–1890. Figures for 1900 and 1910 are exact.

[3] Decrease.

To summarize the point, while the Negro population has become a smaller relative part of the total population each decade since 1810, it has shown a decided trend toward a large actual increase. The distribution of the Negro population has varied with its increase and with the growth of the city. But almost from the beginning, probably the environing white group has segregated the Negroes into separate neighborhoods. The figures available for Brooklyn do not permit a positive inference, but in Manhattan, while the areas populated by Negroes have shifted somewhat from decade to decade, there have been distinctively Colored sections since 1800.[1]

An idea of this segregation is shown in the fact that in 1900, 80.9 per cent of all the Negro population of Manhattan was contained within 12 out of 35 Assembly Districts and that in 1890 seven wards of Manhattan contained fully five-sixths of the Negro population of the Borough. The largest number of Negroes, 13.8 per cent of the total number, were living, in 1900, in the Nineteenth Assembly District with numbers approximating this in the Eleventh, which contained 10.4 per cent, the Twenty-seventh, which had 9.2 per cent, and the Twenty-third, which had 8.7 per cent of the Negro population. The Negro population for Manhattan, 36,246, was distributed in 1900 by assembly districts as is shown in Table IX (p. 49).

These figures give a clear idea of the segregated character of the Negro population and show something of its present location. There has been a decided shifting from the part of Manhattan between Twenty-fifth, Forty-second streets, Sixth and Eighth avenues, and into Harlem between One Hundred and Thirtieth, One Hundred and Fortieth streets, Fifth and Eighth avenues during the past

[1] *Vide* DuBois, *Notes, etc.*, p. 1.

TABLE IX.   DISTRIBUTION OF NEGRO POPULATION BY ASSEMBLY DISTRICTS OF
MANHATTAN, 1900.

Assembly District.	Negro population.	Per cent of total.
5th Assembly District	1,378	3.8
9th Assembly District	1,673	4.6
11th Assembly District	3,756	10.4
13th Assembly District	2,584	7.1
17th Assembly District	1,214	3.4
19th Assembly District	4,982	13.8
21st Assembly District	1,135	3.1
23rd Assembly District	3,169	8.7
25th Assembly District	2,950	8.1
27th Assembly District	3,318	9.2
31st Assembly District	1,483	4.1
32nd Assembly District	1,680	4.6
All other Districts	6,924	19.1
Total	36,246	100.

five years as business interests have been taking possession
of the zone around the new Pennsylvania Railway Station,
between Thirty-second and Thirty-third streets.   But as
the Negroes have moved into blocks in Harlem, the whites
have moved out.

The exact character and extent of the segregation of the
Negro population may be clearly seen from diagrams of
this Harlem district, and of the " San Juan Hill " district
in the West Sixties, based upon the latest figures of the
Census of 1910.   This is given in Diagrams III and IV
(pp. 50-51).[1]

With such a distribution of the clearly segregated Negro
population, the representative character of the 2,500 families chosen for closer study becomes evident.   These families, from figures based upon the original returns of the
New York State Census of 1905, were chosen from the

[1] Diagrams III and IV were made by Mr. Eugene K. Jones, Field
Secretary of the National League on Urban Conditions Among Negroes.

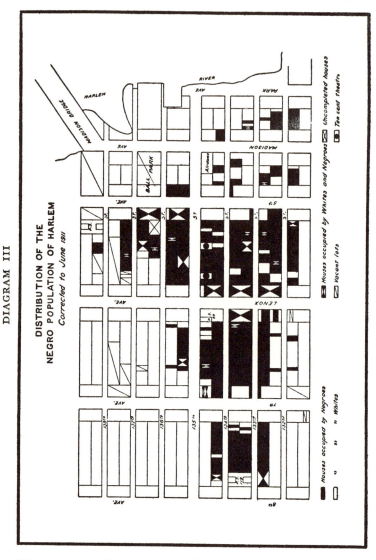

DIAGRAM III

DISTRIBUTION OF THE
NEGRO POPULATION OF HARLEM
Corrected to June 1911

Eleventh, the Nineteenth, the Twenty-third, and the Thirty-
first districts. The last district was taken in preference to

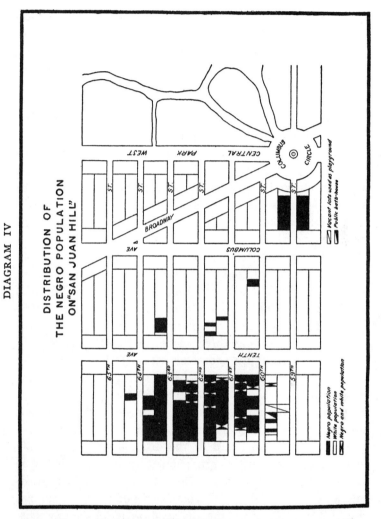

several which contained larger numbers, because it included certain streets that were typical of the Harlem section.

In all 2,639 families were tabulated. Of these 95 were excluded because the heads of these families were of the professional or business classes, 37 because they were too incompletely reported, and 7 because the heads were white. This reduced the number to 2,500 families, which consisted of 9,788 persons, exclusive of 17 white members of these families. The data from the State Census schedules of enumerators were tabulated in regular order as reported by them for each block or part of block for the Negro families that were designated as living in that street or block.

The families studied were from the following territory: Within the Eleventh Assembly District, the area bounded by Thirtieth and Thirty-eighth streets, Seventh and Tenth avenues; within the Nineteenth Assembly District, Sixty-first, Sixty-second, and Sixty-third streets, between Amsterdam and Eleventh avenues, commonly called "San Juan Hill; " within the Twenty-third and Thirty-first Assembly Districts, One Hundred and Thirtieth and One Hundred and Thirty-third streets between Eighth and St. Nicholas avenues, and One Hundred and Thirty-fourth and One Hundred and Thirty-fifth streets between Fifth and Seventh avenues. These three segregated neighborhoods in 1905 may be roughly characterized as follows: The first was probably in the lowest grade of social condition; the second did not show a decidedly predominant type, but ranged from the middle grade toward the more advanced; the third was the most advanced.

A comparison in detail of the distribution by assembly districts of the total Negro population and of the 2,500 selected families shows also that the latter are representative of the several neighborhoods and of the total population. Table X shows the distribution by Assembly Districts of the 2,500 families for comparison with Table IX above, which gave the total Negro population of Manhattan and its distribution.

TABLE X. DISTRIBUTION BY ASSEMBLY DISTRICTS OF 2,500 NEGRO FAMILIES, STATE CENSUS, 1905.

Assembly District.	No. of families.	No. of persons.
Eleventh	927	3,329
Nineteenth	1,018	4,024
Twenty-third.......................	326	1,581
Thirty-first........................	229	854
Total	2,500	9,788

In addition to the data of the State Census of 1905, a personal canvass was made in 1909 of 73 families in their homes, having a total of 212 persons. To these were added 153 individuals at one of the evening schools of the city, a total of 365 persons. The localities within which these 365 people lived corresponded in the main to the location of the 2,500 families taken from the State Census of 1905; that is, between Twenty-fifth, Forty-fifth streets, Fifth and Eighth Avenues; Fifty-third, Sixty-fifth streets, west of Sixth Avenue and between One Hundred and Thirtieth and One Hundred and Thirty-sixth streets, Fifth and Seventh Avenues.

To sum up: The assembly districts chosen and the number of families and individuals tabulated from each district are such as to give a fairly accurate description of the clearly segregated wage-earning Negro population of the districts. The study, then, is representative of about one-fourth of the Negro population of Manhattan in 1905, and is so distributed as to be reasonably conclusive for the wage-earning element of the whole Negro population.

The next question is the composition of this toiling Negro population. The general condition of the wage-earning element of this group will now, therefore, engage our attention.

CHAPTER III

GENERAL CONDITION OF WAGE-EARNERS [1]

I. SEX AND AGE OF NEGRO WAGE-EARNERS

In the 2,500 families composed of 9,788 individuals, the sex distribution and age grouping [2] throw some light upon the life conditions of the wage-earning class. That city life does not look with favor upon a large juvenile element in the population is generally believed. That the city draws mainly those of the working period of life is also generally conceded. The number of children in this Negro group under 15 years of age is 19 per cent, below normal for great cities, and the upper age limit is also quite low, being only 6.6 per cent between forty-five and fifty-four years, and 3.2 per cent over fifty-five years. Thus the bulk of the population, 70.8 per cent, both male and female, excluding 0.4 per cent doubtful and unknown, falls between fifteen and fifty-four years, or within the vigorous working period of life. This is fully set forth in Table XI, which gives the sex distribution and age grouping in assembly districts of the 9,788 individuals in these 2,500 families of the Census of 1905:

[1] The term "wage-earner", for want of a better, is used to designate the group of persons belonging to families whose heads are actual wage-workers. This includes children and some other family members not in gainful occupations.

[2] *Cf.* Bailey, *Modern Social Conditions*, (New York, 1906), pp. 67-89.

TABLE XI. SEX DISTRIBUTION AND AGE GROUPING OF 9,788 NEGRO WAGE-EARNERS IN MANHATTAN, STATE CENSUS, 1905.

Age group.	Male.		Female.		Total.	
	No.	Per cent	No.	Per cent	No.	Per cent
Less than 15 years	949	19.6	910	18.4	1859	19.0
15–24	988	20.4	1155	23.4	2143	21.9
25–34..................	1543	31.8	1546	31.2	3089	31.6
35–44..................	889	18.4	809	16.4	1698	17.3
45–54..................	333	6.9	311	6.3	644	6.6
55 and over	128	2.6	188	3.8	316	3.2
Doubtful and unknown ...	14	0.3	25	0.5	39	0.4
Totals	4844	100.	4944	100.	9788	100.

Figures obtained from the personal canvass made in 1909 bear comparison with those of the State Census of 1905. Substantial agreement is to be noted between the two enumerations, except for the larger percentage of those under 15 years of age in 1905 (19.6 per cent male, 18.4 per cent female), and the smaller percentages in the grouping thirty-five to forty-four years (18.4 per cent male, 16.4 per cent female). Doubtless this effect is produced because so many of the cases in 1909 were individuals attending evening school, who were required to be above 14 years of age, and because few over forty-five years of age are attracted to such a place. The other small difference in percentages is due probably to the small number of individuals, 365, in the figures for 1909. The sex distribution and age grouping in 1909 is shown in Table XII, which follows:

TABLE XII. SEX DISTRIBUTION AND AGE GROUPING OF 365 NEGRO WAGE-
EARNERS IN MANHATTAN, 1909.

Age group.	Male.		Female.		Total.	
	No.	Per cent	No.	Per cent	No.	Per cent
Less than 15 years	18	10.2	21	11.2	39	10.7
15–24.................	35	19.8	37	19.7	72	19.7
25–34.................	54	30.5	50	26.6	104	28.5
35–44.................	40	22.6	41	21.8	81	22.2
45–54.................	11	6.2	21	11.2	32	8.8
55 and over	10	5.6	4	2.1	14	3.8
Doubtful and unknown...	9	5.1	14	7.4	23	6.3
Totals	177	100.	188	100.	365	100.

The results above correspond also with those of the
United States Census of 1900 for the entire City of New
York. Making allowance for some families of professional
and business classes, probably not excluded from the Census figures for 1900, and for changes which five years inter-
val may have caused, the agreement with the two preceding
tables above confirms the representative character of the
data for 1905 and 1909. For the total per cent under fifteen years in 1900 was 19.8; in 1905, 19.0; from fifteeen
to twenty-four years, 24 per cent in 1900, 21.9 per cent in
1905; from twenty-five to thirty-four years, 25.9 per cent
in 1900, 31.6 per cent in 1905; from thirty-five to forty-
four years, 16.2 per cent in 1900, 17.3 per cent in 1905;
from forty-five to fifty-four years, 8.3 per cent in 1900,
6.6 per cent in 1905, and fifty-five years and over, 5.6 per
cent in 1900, 3.2 per cent in 1905.[1]

[1] *Cf.* Twelfth Census, *Bulletin 8, Negroes in the United States,*
Table 31.

Here, then, is a wage-earning group made up of persons in the younger and more vigorous working period. The small number of children under 15 years of age calls attention to the fact that the growth of this population takes place largely through recruits from other sections of the Country. They must find industrial and social adjustment to a new environment largely made up of the white population. They are either killed off by the conditions under which they work and live, or drift away from the city at a premature old age.

2. NATIVITY OF NEGRO WAGE-EARNERS

If New York has a Negro population largely composed of immigrants from other regions, the question naturally arises, From what sections or regions do they come? The State Census of 1905 gives nativity by countries only. Consequently, those born within the United States are not specified by State or territory of birth. That large numbers of the Negro population of New York City come from other sections of the United States, mainly from the South, is beyond doubt.

We get the first impression of this fact from the Federal Census of 1900. For the whole State of New York in 1900, out of a population of 100,000,[1] 44.6 per cent were natives, 24.1 per cent were from Virginia, 19 per cent were from other Southern States, with a remaining 12.3 per cent to be drawn from other parts of the United States and from other countries.

These proportions are different from those for New York City, because immigrants make up a larger part of the City's Negro population. The figures of the State Census of 1905, as well as those from a personal canvass,

---

[1] DuBois, *Notes, etc.*, p. 2.

point in the same direction, and the evidence indicates clearly the probable condition.

The West Indian element in the Negro population of the City was noticed first. The British West Indies furnish 5.8 per cent of these foreign Negro immigrants, while the Danish West Indies, Cuba, and those islands not specified, together make up 3.6 per cent, a total of 9.4 per cent West Indian.[1] Table XIII (p. 59) gives a survey of this part of the population and shows its relation to the native born.

We are unable to get from the figures of Table XIII the sections or States of the United States from which the 89.5 per cent of American-born Negroes came. The few straws of evidence afforded by the personal canvass point to the main sources of the stream. The percentages have significance although the figures are few. The Southern States, from which there are easy means of transportation to New York, naturally furnish the larger part. Virginia supplied 29.6 per cent of the 365 Manhattan residents; South Carolina, 11 per cent; Georgia, 6 per cent, and Maryland, 4.4 per cent. Taking the Southern States by themselves, 67.5 per cent of the 365 wage-earners were born in that section. Besides 5.7 per cent of the 365

[1] In a study of *Negro Craftsmen in New York City* made by Miss Helen A. Tucker in 1907 (*Vide, Southern Workman,* 1907, 36: 9, p. 550), she reported the most reliable estimate of the proportion of West Indians in New York City as about one-tenth of the total Negro population. The figures above substantiate such an estimate. Of the 385 men in Miss Tucker's study, 29.09 per cent were born in the West Indies. Among the 94 who claimed to know a trade, 57 or 60.64 per cent were born in the West Indies. *Cf. ibid.,* 37: 1, p. 45. This wide variation of percentage from that given for 9,788 individuals in 1905, probably arises because (1) of the larger number of cases in the latter instance, (2) the returns are from two other districts of Manhattan besides "the Sixties" of Miss Tucker's canvass, (3) Miss Tucker canvassed male craftsmen only; the figures of this text cover the whole population.

TABLE XIII. NATIVITY BY COUNTRY OF BIRTH OF 9,788 WAGE-EARNERS, MANHATTAN, 1905.

Country of birth.	No.	No.	Per cent
The Bermudas	..	28	0.3
British West Indies	..	566	5.8
Antiqua	1	..	..
Bahama Islands	7	..	..
Barbadoes	36	..	..
Jamaica	19	..	..
St. Croix	46	..	..
St. Christopher	20	..	..
St. Thomas	8	..	..
Trinidad	1	..	..
Not specified	428	..	..
Danish West Indies	..	62	0.6
Cuba	..	14	0.1
West Indies (not specified)	..	285	2.9
Canada	..	16	0.2
United States	..	8757	89.5
Miscellaneous [1]	..	36	0.4
Unknown	..	24	0.2
Total	..	9,788	100.

came from the British West Indies. The West Indies and the Southern States probably furnished 73.4 per cent or about three-fourths of these wage-earners in the Negro population of New York City. Table XIV (p. 60) shows in full the State and country of birth of the 365 wage-earners.

Foreign and native immigrants predominate in the Negro population of the City. With such a stream of immigrants the question arises about their marriage and family relationships. Are they largely single people, or are there large numbers of married, widowed, or divorced persons among them? The discussion next centers upon this point.

[1] The miscellaneous includes the following: Australia 3, England 7, East Indies 1, France 1, Germany 1, Hayti 1, India 2, Ireland 1, Mexico 2, Monrovia, Africa 1, Porto Rico 9, Sandwich Islands 1, Santo Domingo 2, South America 4.

TABLE XIV.—NATIVITY BY STATE OR COUNTRY OF BIRTH OF 365 WAGE
EARNERS, MANHATTAN, 19C9.

Country.	No.	Per cent	No.	Per cent	Country.	No.	Per cent	No.	Per cent
Bermuda	..	..	4	1.1	United States	....	....	307	84.2
					Georgia	22	6.0	....	....
British West Indies	..	..	21	5.7	Maryland	16	4.4	....	....
Antigua	3	..	..	....	New York	40	11.0	....	....
Barbadoes	8	..	..	....	North Carolina	35	9.6	....	....
Grenada	1	..	..	....	South Carolina	40	11.0	....	....
Jamaica	1	..	..	....	Virginia	108	29.6	....	....
Nassau	1	..	..	....	Other States [1]	46	12.6	....	....
St. Croix	3	..	..	....	Miscellaneous [2]	....	....	4	1.1
St. Kitts	1	..	..	....	Unknown	....	....	29	7.9
Trinidad	1	..	..	....					
Island Unknown	2	..	..	....	Total	....	....	365	100

3. MARITAL CONDITION OF WAGE-EARNERS

The State Census of 1905 did not ask about the marital
condition, but only stated relationships to the head of the
family, so that the conjugal condition of women reported
as heads of families, of lodgers, and of adult sons and
daughters or other relatives in the family could not be ascertained. Therefore, no attempt was made to give statements about conjugal condition based on these returns.
However, in the personal canvass of 326 individuals, fifteen years of age and over, the marital condition was obtained. The small number of cases included in Table XV
makes the figures and percentages presented valuable for
pointing only to what a larger body of data would probably make certain. It is important, therefore, to note that
113 out of 159 males, or 71.1 per cent, and 106 out of 167
females, or 63.5 per cent, were single, excluding those un-

[1] The other states of the Union are: Alabama 2, Arkansas 2, Delaware 2, Dis-
trict of Columbia 7, Florida 7, Illinois 1, Kentucky 4, Massachusetts 4, Missouri 3,
Ohio 2, Pennsylvania 3, Tennessee 2, Texas 2, Michigan 1, New Jersey 1, Rhode
Island 1, Porto Rico 2.

[2] Miscellaneous: St. Martin 1, Ontario 1, British Guiana 2.

known. This suggests what the age grouping would lead us to expect, viz., that the Negro group in New York City has a large proportion of unmarried persons. Table XV, which follows, indicates this conclusion:

TABLE XV. MARITAL CONDITION OF 326 NEGRO WAGE-EARNERS, FIFTEEN YEARS OF AGE AND OVER, MANHATTAN, 1909.

Marital condition.	Male.		Female.		Total.	
	No.	Per cent	No.	Per cent	No.	Per cent
Married................	26	16.3	30	17.9	56	17.2
Single	113	71.1	106	63.5	219	67.2
Widowed	9	5.7	27	16.2	36	11.0
Divorced	3	1.9	....	....	3	0.9
Unknown	8	5.0	4	2.4	12	3.7
Total	159	100.	167	100.	326	100.

Now that the marital condition of the individuals has been indicated, we may profitably inquire into the composition of the families.

4. FAMILIES AND LODGERS

An illuminating sidelight is thrown upon the general condition of wage-earners by a study of the sizes of families and the relation of lodgers to those families. The figures used are those of the State Census of 1905 only, as the number of complete families secured in the personal canvass was too small. The points of importance are the size of the economic family, which includes lodgers and all others living under one head, and size of the natural family when lodgers are excluded. The census returns of 1905 showed relationship of each dweller in the household to the head of the family. It was thus easy to separate lodgers, except in some cases when relatives may have been lodgers but were not so designated. Taking the 2,500 families as a whole, with 9,788 individuals, the average size of the family was three and nine-tenths persons. Of these, 2,631 individuals, 26.9 per cent were lodgers, and 7,157, or 73.1 per cent, were natural members. But these aggregates do not portray actual conditions. A true picture may be obtained from a more detailed study of the figures which show that 119, or 4.8 per cent, of the economic families (which includes all persons living under one head) consisted of an individual living alone; 576, 23 per cent, of two persons; 531, 21.2 per cent, of the families had three members, while 478, 19.1 per cent, were composed of four members. Above four, the percentages of families rapidly declined; 13.4 per cent of economic families had five members; 8.3 per cent, six members; 5 per cent, seven members, down to 2.2 per cent, eight members; 1.4 per cent, nine members, and 1.6 per cent, ten or more members. But the composition of these economic families is even more striking. To illustrate, of a total of 576 economic families with two members, 488 had no lodgers, and this was 36.1 per cent of all the families without lodgers; out of 531 families of three members each, 173 had one lodger, or 37.7 per cent of all families having one lodger, and 67 families had two lodgers each, or 20.6 per cent of all the families having two lodgers. Further, 478 families of four members each contained 133 families with two lodgers, 40.9 per cent of all families having two lodgers, and 48 families had three lodgers, 27 per cent of all families having three lodgers, while only 84 families had one lodger, and 213 families, less than one-half, 44.6 per cent of all families of four members each, had no lodgers. Taking the entire 2,500 families, only 1,353 families, or 54.1 per cent, had no lodgers; 459, or 18.4 per cent of the total families, had one lodger only; 325 families, or 13 per cent of the total, had two lodgers only, while 320 families, or 12.8 per cent of the total, had from 3 to 5 lodgers. This left 45, or 1.7 per cent, with 6 to 9 lodgers. In a phrase, the increase in the size of the family means, as a rule, an increase in the number of lodgers, and the relative proportion of natural members probably decreases as the size of the family increases, the proportion of lodgers increasing with the size of the economic family.

Now this showing is not the effect of lodging-houses run as business enterprises, except probably in the families ten members or more, which constitute only 1.6 per cent of the total 2,500 families. This condition is most probably due in part to the fact—which both Census returns and personal observation indicated but could not fully determine—that many of the lodgers consisted of married couples, sometimes with one or two children, and of parts of broken families. Furthermore, the high rents [1] which Negroes have to pay, the limited area in which the opposition of whites allows them to live, together with the small income power due to the occupational field being largely restricted to domestic and personal service, play a large part in forcing families and parts of families to live thus crowded together. This last point about income will be referred to again in Chapter IV on Occupations and in Chapter V on Wages. It is a cause for serious concern that only 54.1 per cent of the families had no lodgers, and this percentage

---

[1] Real estate agents, who have handled properties during the change from white to Negro tenants, testified that Negro families upon moving in pay from $2.00 to $5.00 more per apartment. Others corroborated their statements. *Vide* also, Chapin, *Standard of Living in New York City*, pp. 76-77.

here will probably hold for the entire Negro population of the City. If we exclude the 119 individuals living alone, the families having no lodgers fall to 51.8 per cent.

This last phase of the lodger condition is emphasized if presented in another way which shows the number of families having a specified number of members, exclusive of lodgers. For the same 2,500 families, it brings out from another point of view the relation of the family to the lodgers. There is presented both the number and percent of families that had a specified number of lodgers, and also, the number and percent of families that had a specified number of members exclusive of lodgers. For example, 178 families had three lodgers each, which was 7.1 per cent of the total 2,500 families. And of these 48 families had only one other member; 57 had two other members; 36 had three other; 23 four other; 9 five other; 3 six other, and 1 seven other. Out of 1,353 families that did not accommodate lodgers, 898 families, 67.8 per cent, had three members or less. Of 1,147 families that did accommodate lodgers, 606, 52.8 per cent, had more lodgers than natural members. And if we take the totals, 392, 15.7 per cent, of the families had besides lodgers only one natural member; 909, 36.4 per cent, of the families had in addition to lodgers two members only, and 508, 20.3 per cent, had besides lodgers three members only; 329 families, 13.2 per cent of the total, had four natural members; 325, 12.9 per cent, had five to seven natural members, and 38, 1.5 per cent, had eight or more natural members. This makes it clear that 1,809 of the 2,500 families had three natural members or less, if lodgers are not counted. To take a statement in a percentage that probably will be applicable to the whole City, one may say that, even including relatives who may have been lodgers, 72.6 per cent of Negro families had three members or less, if the lodgers are excluded—a fact of almost startling social significance. All this is a cause for serious concern, and any constructive steps for social betterment should give attention to the causes and remedies for this condition as one of the first and most urgent problems.

To sum up the general condition of wage-earners: The Negro population has increased decade by decade, except from 1840 to 1850 and from 1850 to 1860, preceding and during the Abolition and Civil War crisis. It is made up of young persons and adults in the vigorous working period, and has a small number of children under fifteen years of age. The population is recruited largely by immigrants from the South and the West Indies, who do not survive or remain in the City to a very old age. Among the wage-earners probably single people predominate. Largely because of high rents and low incomes, lodgers made up of married couples, parts of broken families and of individuals seriously interfere with normal family life. The families are usually very small in size, from two to four persons, and an increase in the size of the family generally means an increase in the number of lodgers.

CHAPTER IV

Occupations of Wage-earners

I. AN HISTORICAL VIEW OF OCCUPATIONS

In the New Amsterdam Colony as early as 1628, slaves were sought as a source of labor. These slaves were employed mainly in farm labor. In that year the Dutch West India Company agreed to furnish slaves to the colonists and the Company's largest farm was "cultivated by the blacks." [1] Individuals were at liberty to import slaves for the same purpose. [2] Both slaves and freedmen were used as stevedores and deckhands for the Company's vessels. The slaves were also used in building and repairing the public highways and in the repairing of Fort Amsterdam. [3] In 1680, mention is made of Negroes being used in house-building. [4] About the same time Negro slaves were carrying hod for wages, and in 1699 it was said that about the only servants (probably meaning domestic servants) in the Province of New York were Negroes. Freed Negroes were indentured or hired for similar service. [5]

Negroes were mustered into the Colonial army as early as 1698, and in the battle of Lake George in 1755, the "blacks behaved better than the whites." [6]

[1] Williams, *History of the Negro Race in America*, vol. i, p. 135.

[2] *Colonial Doc.*, i, 364.

[3] *Laws of New York*, 1691-1773, pp. 83, 156; *Doc. relating to Colonial History of New York*, vol. i, 499; ii, 474.

[4] *Doc. relating to Colonial History of New York*, iii, 307.

[5] *Ibid.*, ix, 875; iv, 511; Burghermen and Freemen, *collection of New York Historical Society*, 1885, p. 569.

[6] *Ibid.*, 377 (London Doc. xi); *ibid.*, vi, 1005 (London Doc. xxxii.) "Letter from a gunner to his cousin."

66   [502

Under the Dutch government enfranchised and slave Negroes were allowed to acquire and hold land. Some took advantage of this privilege. But with English possession of the colony it was expressly prohibited.[1] Some few Negroes were seamen as shown by the records of the so-called Negro plot of 1741, and one Negro doctor, Harry by name, was among those executed during the time of that insane public excitement.[2]

From about 1835 until 1841 a weekly newspaper, *The Colored American,* owned and published by Charles B. Ray, Philip A. Bell and others, was published in New York. It had an extensive circulation from Boston to Cincinnati. From this source a number of employments and business enterprises of Negroes in the New York of that period were ascertained. The occupations included three carpenters and joiners, five boot and shoe-makers, five tailors, two music teachers, four teachers of private and evening schools, one newspaper agent, one engraver, one watch and clock-maker, one sign-painter, two dress and cloak makers.[3]

In this period between 1830 and 1860, there were many engaged in domestic and personal service. Most of the smaller hotels of the times had colored waiters. The Metropolitan had about 60 or 70; other hostelries like the Stuyvesant House, the Earls, the Clifford, and a number of restaurants employed colored waiters. Some cooks and barbers, who also applied leeches, treated corns, and did other minor surgical services, were among this class of wage-earners.

Three dentists, P. H. White, John Burdell, and Joshua Bishop, two physicians, James McCune Smith and W. M.

---

[1] Williams, *op. cit.,* pp. 137, 142.

[2] Horsmanden, *History of the Negro Plot, passim.*

[3] For business enterprises, see chap. v, pp. 96-7.

Lively, and three ministers, H. W. Garnet, Chas. B. Ray, and Peter Williams, were prominent persons of the period

But these facts should not give the impression of unalloyed opportunity in the trades and professions, for the columns of this same Negro newspaper were filled with articles, editorials and appeals which indicate the difficulties in that direction. This is further borne out by the testimony of Charles S. Andrews, the white principal of the Manumission Society School for Negroes. He said his graduates left with every avenue closed against them and spoke of difficulties those who had trades encountered, many being forced to become waiters, barbers, servants, and laborers.[1] That domestic and personal service furnished employment for a large number of Negroes is further shown by the organization of the United Public Waiters' Mutual Beneficial Association. This effort was first started by twelve Negro caterers as a corporation to control and keep up the quality of service both by looking after the efficiency of the many waiters they employed and by preventing " irresponsible men attempting to cater at weddings, balls, parties, and some hotels on special occasions." Originally their constitution, framed in 1869, stated the objects of the organization to be " to consolidate the business interests of its members; to encourage and promote industrial pursuits followed by them; to give preference in patronage to its members." [2]

Five of the original corporators, among whom were George Morris, George E. Green, and Charles W. Hopewell, owned imported silver, china, and other caterers' " service " ranging in valuation from about $1,000 to $4,000, and all of them had ability to manage large banquets and other social functions, supplying waiters, cooks, etc. First smaller caterers, then waiters, were taken into

---

[1] Quoted in Ovington, *Half a Man*, pp. 27-28.

[2] *Constitution and By-Laws of the United Public Waiters' Mutual Beneficial Association.*

the organization until the membership increased to more than a hundred. And in 1872 they added the mutual benefit features, " to insure both medical and brotherly aid when sick and to assist respectably interring its deceased members." One of the caterers of the early corporation, W. E. Gross, is yet in the business at the Bowery Savings Bank and still serves for special occasions, now mainly among Colored people. The organization as a benefit association continued with varying fortunes down to 1905, when it was dissolved by its remaining 33 members.

That there were many other waiters and servants of the time is certain. A head-waiter of that day estimated the number of colored hotel and restaurant waiters at between 400 and 500 in 1870.

2. OCCUPATIONS IN 1890 AND 1900

By the time of the Federal censuses of 1890 and 1900 the Negro population in New York had grown to considerable proportions, and for this increased population we are fortunate in having full occupational returns. Although these figures included all persons ten years of age and over, those under fourteen years probably formed a negligible part of the totals because the Child Labor Laws of the State of New York prohibited the employment of children under fourteen years of age.

It appears, as was expected, that the large majority of Negro wage-earners were engaged in domestic and personal service. But it is significant that in 1890 there were among the male population 236 bookkeepers, accountants, etc., 476 draymen, hackmen, and teamsters, and 427 were engaged in manufacturing and mechanical pursuits. Among the females, there were 418 dressmakers, 103 seamstresses, and 67 nurses and midwives.

The figures for 1900 show a large percentage of increase in domestic and personal service. In occupations classed under trade and transportation, Negro wage-earners increased 450.3 per cent compared with an increase of 177.2

per cent among native whites. Nor is this increase due entirely to semi-personal service occupations for the class of clerks, bookkeepers, etc., had increased from 236 in 1890 to 456 in 1900; draymen, hackmen, and teamsters numbered 1,439 in 1900 as compared with 476 in 1890, an increase of 202.3 per cent. In manufacturing and mechanical pursuits the percentage of increase during the ten years, 1890 to 1900, was 140.3 per cent, larger than that of the native whites, 137.3 per cent. Only one occupation in this class had a smaller increase of Negro workers than 75 per cent. Machinists increased from 7 to 47; brick and stone masons from 20 to 94, or 370 per cent; stationary engineers and firemen from 61 to 227, or 271.1 per cent. Other comparisons indicate clearly a similarly favorable advance in many occupations other than domestic and personal service. Large allowances, of course, must be made for the errors in gathering the figures of the two censuses; yet this does not account for all of the decided increases shown. It must be accounted for on the ground that slowly the walls of inefficiency on one side and of prejudice on the other which have confined Negroes to the more menial and lower-paid employments are being broken down. This progress has come in the face of the fact that the more ambitious and efficient individual is " tied to his group." [1]

In 1890 and 1900 a large number of occupations could not be included in the table because the figures for 1890 were not available. The comparison of the two censuses shows clearly that there is for Negro wage-earners a probable enlargement of the scope of occupations outside of domestic and personal service.

Table XVI below gives in detail the number and percent of increase of the native white and Negro wage-earners, ten years of age and over, engaged in selected occupations in New York City in 1890 and 1900:

[1] Ovington, *op. cit.*, pp. 93-95.

TABLE XVI. NATIVE WHITE AND NEGRO WAGE-EARNERS, TEN YEARS OF AGE AND OVER, ENGAGED IN SELECTED OCCUPATIONS, NEW YORK CITY, 1890 AND 1900.[1]

| | Male. | | | | | |
| | Native white. | | | Negro. | | |
Occupation.	1890.	1900.	Per cent increase.	1890	1900.	Per cent increase.
Domestic and personal service..	16,887	42,621	152.4	4,975	27,956	461.9
Barbers and hairdressers	1,017	1,936	60.9	111	215	....
Bartenders	2,530	5,776	128.3	29	84	....
Janitors and sextons	712	2,037	186.2	336	800	118.6
Laborers (not classified)	8,807	26,669	203.1	882	3,719	352.4
[2] Servants and waiters	3,821	6,473	69.4	3,647	6,280	72.2
Trade and transportation	69,162	170,350	146.3	1,520	5,338	450.3
Boatmen and sailors	1,024	3,675	258.9	106	145	36.8
[6]Bookkeepers and accountants	34,960	16,526	......	236	33	....
Clerks and copyists	......	62,921	......	....	423	....
Draymen, hackmen, teamsters, etc.	12,908	31,695	145.5	476	1,439	202.3
[3]Hostlers	840	1,659	......	100	633	....
[4]Messengers, errand and office boys..................	} 7,711	{ 10,578	} 117.4	559 {	355	} 347.4
Packers and shippers........		2,026			23	
Porters and helpers (in stores)		4,157			2,143	
Salesmen.................	8,398	29,889	255.9	15	94	526.7
Steam railroad employees....	3,321	7,224	121.1	28	70	150.0
Manufacturing and mechanical pursuits	30,180	71,613	137.3	427	1,026	140.3
Blacksmiths	1,169	2,490	113.0	9	29	....
Masons (brick and stone) ...	2,278	5,032	120.1	20	94	370.0
Painters, glaziers and varnishers.	5,805	12,947	123.0	99	177	78.8
Plasterers	701	1,592	127.1	10	51	410.0
Plumbers, gas and steam fitters	5,225	12,355	136.4	11	31	....
Carpenters and joiners	4,712	11,471	143.4	33	94	184.8
Tobacco and cigar factory operatives	1,940	2,182	12.0	146	189	29.4
Tailors..................	2,200	4,545	106.6	20	69	245.0
Upholsterers	860	1,447	68.2	11	18	63.3
Engineers and firemen (not locomotive)	2,622	8,129	210.0	61	227	272.1
Machinists	2,368	9,423	297.9	7	47	....
Total	116,224	284,584	144.8	6,922	34,321	395.8

TABLE XVI.—*Concluded.*

Occupation.	Female.					
	Native white.			Negro.		
	1890.	1900.	Per cent increase.	1890.	1900.	Per cent increase.
Musicians and teachers of music.	950	2,581	171.7	24	73	204.2
Housekeepers and stewardesses.	797	2,421	203.8	83	226	172.3
Laundresses	1,416	4,329	205.7	1,526	3,224	111.3
Nurses and midwives., ...	1,220	4,416	262.0	67	290	332.8
5 Servants and waitresses	11,140	22,616	103.0	3,754	10,297	174.3
Clerks and copyists	2,505	7,811	419.0	5	22	....
Bookkeepers and accountants ..	1,492	6,998	360.0	2	10	....
Stenographers and typewriters..	1,356	9,518	601.9	3	14	....
Saleswomen	7,476	18,315	144.7	4	13	....
Dressmakers	13,106	22,137	68.9	418	813	94.5
Seamstresses	4,206	7,855	86.7	103	249	141.7
Total	45,664	108,997	138.5	5,989	15,231	154.3

OCCUPATIONS IN 1905

In the 2,500 families, composed of 9,788 persons, 1,859 were excluded because of their being under fifteen years of age and 82 were excluded because, although members of wage-earning families, they themselves were either in a professional occupation, or were engaged in a business

NOTES FOR TABLE XVI.

[1] Eleventh Census, *Part ii, Population,* p. 704. Occupations for Negroes in 1890 are approximately accurate as Chinese, etc., made up less than 10 per cent. of the total Colored population. Twelfth Census, *Special Rep.,* Table 43, *Occupations,* pp. 634–640.

[2] In 1890 occupation marked only "servants."

[3] Includes livery-stable keepers in 1890.

[4] Messengers, packers, and porters, etc., classed together in 1890.

[5] 1900, "servants and waitresses;" 1890, "servants."

[6] Includes clerks, etc., in 1890.

enterprise on their own account. This left 7,847 individual wage-earners, 3,802 of whom were male and 4,045 were female. Both the male and the female wage-earners show a very large percentage employed in domestic and personal service, 40.2 per cent male and 89.3 per cent female, a large percentage of whom doubtless were married women and widows with children.[1] But it is to be noted as important that among the males, 20.6 per cent were engaged in some occupation classified under Trade and 9.4 per cent under Transportation. While some of these occupations may differ little in character from domestic and personal service, yet the occupations that are entirely removed from that classification are sufficient in number to show, as did the figures for 1890 and 1900, the possibility of Negroes in considerable numbers securing a scope of employment which includes other occupations than those of domestic and personal service.

The State Census figures are more detailed than those of the Federal Census. For example, under domestic and personal service, the Federal Census has grouped together male waiters and servants, while the State Census figures have been tabulated separately. It is also probable that the classification in 1890 and 1900 included wage-earners who were classified differently in 1905 and *vice versa*. And in 1905 professional occupations as well as all persons doing business on their own account were excluded. Differences in the figures may, therefore, be allowed.

Table XVII, which follows, shows the latest figures available on the scope of employment of Negro wage-earners:

---

[1] *Cf.* Ovington, *op. cit.*, pp. 56-57, 144-145.

TABLE XVII.   OCCUPATIONS OF NEGRO WAGE-EARNERS, FIFTEEN YEARS OF AGE
AND OVER, MANHATTAN, 1905.[1]

MALE

Occupation.	Totals.	No.	Per cent
Public service	55	..	1.4
Sailors and mariners (U. S.)..................	....	3	....
Federal employees custom house, immigration, etc.)	....	6	....
Post office (clerks)...........................	....	13	....
Post office (carriers).........................	....	9	....
Street cleaning department	....	23	....
Miscellaneous.................................	....	1	....
Domestic and personal service	1,527	..	40.2
Barbers......................................	....	27	....
Bartenders	....	24	....
Bellmen and doormen	....	154	4.0
Bootblacks	....	2	....
Butlers......................................	....	41	....
Chauffeurs	....	9	....
Cleaners (house, etc.)	....	15	....
Coachmen....................................	....	68	1.8
Cooks	....	110	2.9
Cooks (dining car)............................	....	7	....
Chimney sweeps..............................	....	2	....
Domestic servants (not specified)	....	12	....
Elevatormen.................................	....	365	9.6
Hallmen (hotel, etc.).........................	....	90	2.4
Hotel managers...............................	....	3	....
Housemen	....	29	....
Janitors and caretakers........................	....	83	2.2
Stewards	....	38	....
Valets	....	18	....
Waiters......................................	....	425	11.2
Miscellaneous	....	5	....
Manufacturers and mechanical pursuits...........	300	....	7.9
Asphalt layers	....	6	....
Blacksmiths	....	5	....
Carpenters	....	18	....
Confectioners	....	3	....
Drill runners	....	5	....

[1] In classifying these occupations, some departure has been made from the
Federal Census arrangement. Those engaged in Public Service have been separated from Domestic and Personal Service, while Trade and Transportation are
tabulated separately; a few occupations have been put in an unclassified list,
while one or two occupations are included that might possibly be regarded as
professional. This rearrangement, however, does not prevent comparison with
previous Federal Census classification, and it is hoped that it is in line with subsequent classifications.

TABLE XVII.—*Continued*

MALE

Occupation.	Totals.	No.	Per cent
Manufacturers and mechanical pursuits—*Continued.*			
Electricians..	....	3	....
Engineers (not locomotive).....................	....	48	....
Firemen (not locomotive)......................	....	19	....
Factory employees (not specified)	....	6	....
Hodcarriers	....	9	....
Harness and saddlemakers	....	2	....
Cigarmakers......................................	....	32	....
Kalsominers.....................................	....	8	....
Machinists	....	12	....
Mechanics (automobile, bicycle, etc.)	....	9	....
Masons (stone)	....	2	....
Masons (brick)	....	8	....
Masons (not specified)........................	....	5	....
Painters and decorators	....	26	....
Plasterers	....	7	....
Plumbers, steam and gas fitters...............	....	5	....
Printers and compositors	....	14	....
Shoemakers and repairers	....	6	....
Tailors...	....	20	....
Miscellaneous...................................	....	22	....
Trade	783	..	20.6
Agents (real estate)	....	4	....
Bookkeepers	....	3	....
Clerks (office, banks, etc.)....................	....	11	....
Shipping clerks	...	9	....
Clerks and salesmen (in stores, etc.)	....	63	1.7
Laundry employees..............................	....	13	....
Messengers, errand boys and office boys	....	60	1.6
Watchmen	....	10	....
Porters (stores, etc.).........................	....	587	15.4
Stenographers	....	4	....
Miscellaneous	....	19	....
Transportation	359	..	9.4
Boatmen and seamen	....	17	....
Expressmen, truckmen and drivers...............	....	119	3.1
Hostlers and stablemen	....	47	1.2
Longshoremen....................................	....	75	2.0
Porters (railway)	....	83	2.2
Porters (street railway)	....	7	....
Steamship company (not specified)	....	4	....
Street railway (not specified)	....	3	....
Telephone operators............................	....	3	....
Car cleaner.....................................	....	1	....
Unclassified	778	..	20.5
Gardeners.......................................	....	3	....
Laborers (not specified).......................	....	616	16.2
Musicians and musical performers	....	55	1.4
Foremen (not specified)	....	4	....
Theatrical (not specified).....................	....	6	....
Unknown	....	94	....
Total for all occupations	3,802		

TABLE XVII.—*Concluded*

FEMALE

Occupation.	Totals.	No.	Per cent
Domestic and personal service...................	3,456	..	89.3
Chambermaids...............................	....	22	....
Cooks	....	149	....
Day workers out	....	19	....
Domestic servants (not specified)...............	....	88	2.3
Hairdressers................................	....	6	....
Manicurists and masseurs.....................	....	18	....
Housekeepers	....	60	....
Housewives	....	51	....
General housework (wages)	....	720	18.6
General housework (not specified)...............	....	1,572	....
Janitress and caretakers	....	28	....
Laundresses................................	....	543	14.0
Ladies' maids...............................	....	23	....
Maids (not specified).........................	....	80	2.1
Nurses	....	21	....
Waitresses	....	47	....
Miscellaneous...............................	....	4	....
Trade	25	..	0.6
Bookkeepers	....	2	....
Clerks and saleswomen.......................	....	6	....
Stenographers and typewriters..................	....	8	....
Miscellaneous...............................	....	9	....
Manufacturing and mechanical pursuits...........	564	..	5.5
Dressmakers................................	....	164	4.2
Garment workers............................	....	18	.5
Milliners	....	5	....
Seamstresses...............................	....	16	....
Tailors' assistants......	....	3	....
Miscellaneous...............................	....	6	....
Unclassified	176	..	4.6
Telephone operators..........................	....	1	....
Unknown	....	175	....
Total for all occupations..................	4,045	..	....

Before leaving the subject of the restricted scope of occupations among Negroes, something should be said of the far-reaching effects this restriction has upon the life of the wage-earners. Negroes are crowded into these poorer-paid occupations because many of them are inefficient and because of the color prejudice on the part of white workmen and employers.[1] Both of these influences are severe handicaps in the face of the competition in this advanced industrial community.

Restricted thus to a few occupations, there is a larger number of competitors within a limited field with a consequent tendency to lower an already low wage scale. In this way the limitations of occupational mobility react upon income, producing a low standard of living, the lodger evil, and social consequences pointed out below (pp. 80, 89, 144 ff).

To sum up the occupational condition of Negro wage-earners: The large majority of Negroes are employed today in occupations of domestic and personal service. This is partly the result of the historical conditions of servitude, of a prejudice on the part of white workmen and employers, which restricts them to this lower field, and of the inefficiency of Negro wage-earners for competition in occupations requiring a higher order of training and skill. The steady increase in 1890, 1900 and 1905 of numbers employed in occupations other than personal and domestic service is prophetic of a probable widening scope of the field of employment open to them.

[1] In a canvass of business establishments 12 manufacturers, 1 architect, 3 plumbers and steam-fitters, 2 printing firms, 10 contractors and builders and 3 miscellaneous—37 total—12 were decidedly against employing Negroes, 9 giving as a reason the objections of their white workmen; 13 were non-committal, and 12, 10 of whom were builders and contractors, offered or gave employment to Negroes above the average competency; *cf.* Ovington, *op. cit.*, pp. 91-98.

CHAPTER V

WAGES AND EFFICIENCY OF WAGE-EARNERS

THE question of wages and working efficiency are so closely related that they can be better treated together than separately. The material for this part of the monograph has been gathered from three sources, namely: a personal canvass, the records of employment agencies for personal and domestic help, and the statement of union rates published by the New York Bureau of Labor Statistics. It has not been possible to calculate the time loss by the worker, and therefore any estimate of annual income based upon the figures given must be made on the assumption of a full year of work. This, of course, is not the actual case, especially with many wage-earners in domestic and personal service.

I. WAGES IN DOMESTIC AND PERSONAL SERVICE

The Employment Agencies' Law of New York City requires that each agency keep a careful and accurate record of the wages of those for whom they secure situations, as well as written references from former employers of each applicant. Since inspectors from the Bureau of Licenses have access to these records at any time, they are probably carefully kept. The material on wages which has been taken largely from these sources has been arranged to show the number of individuals who receive a specified wage, beginning at less than $4.00 and running by $1.00 groups up to $9.00 and over. There follows (p. 80) a table covering 682 males in twenty-four occupations and 2,138 females in

78   [514

twenty-five occupations from 1906 to 1909. It will be noted that in some cases two occupations are given under one heading such as elevator and switchboard, or cook and laundress. In these cases, the individual is paid the same for the two branches of work; so far as the wage is concerned it is one occupation. It is significant that out of a total of 682 males, 513, or 75.2 per cent, received wages under $6.00 per week and that 141, or 20.7 per cent, received between $6.00 and $8.99 per week, while only 4.1 per cent received $9.00 or more per week. With the females, the showing is even more unfavorable. Out of a total of 2,138 females, 1,971, or 92.2 per cent, received less than $6.00 per week, and of these 1,137, or 53.2 per cent, received less than $5.00 per week. Of those receiving $6.00 or more per week, only 8 out of 2,138, or .04 per cent, received as much as $9.00 or more per week.

Of course, many of these wage-earners are furnished their meals in addition to wages; some have meals and room. In some cases question may arise about the effect of lodgings furnished by the employer upon the wages paid his domestic help, but both from the testimony of the employment agent and from statements made in the records, it does not appear that wages are different whether the servants " sleep in " or " sleep out." There are no data to show whether or not consideration of car-fare had any effect on the wages.

An inspection of the list of occupations for which these wages are given and the fact that they were employed in private families (see Table XVIII below) show that comparatively few of these wage-earners had opportunity to receive any considerable money from tips. This is especially true of the females. We may take, therefore, the figures of the table as probably giving an accurate statement of the wages received in domestic service in New York City during the four years, 1906 to 1909.

When one considers the probable dependents on many of these wage-earners, the high rents and high cost of food, he is not surprised to. find that about half of these families take lodgers (see p. 64), and that a majority of the women are bread-winners (see p. 73). He sees the poorly-paid domestic service on the one side and on the other the cost of living as high walls bounding a narrow, restricted road that leads to a low standard of living and to social and economic disease. Table XVIII shows the picture in full relief:

TABLE XVIII. WEEKLY WAGES BY GROUPS OF WAGE-EARNERS FOR SELECTED OCCUPATIONS IN DOMESTIC AND PERSONAL SERVICE, NEW YORK CITY, 1906–1909.[1]

MALE

Occupations.	Less than $4.00.	$4.00 to $4.99.	$5.00 to $5.99.	$6.00 to $6.99.	$7.00 to $7.99.	$8.00 to $8.99.	$9.00 and over.	Total.
Bartenders.	....	....	....	....	....	....	1	1
Bellmen	3	1	....	....	....	....	....	4
Blacksmiths	1	....	....	....	....	....	1	2
Butlers	.. .	4	18	4	11	4	....	41
Butler and cook	....	1	1	....	1	....	....	3
Coachmen	....	1	2	...	1	....	1	5
Cooks.	....	2	3	1	5	3	14	28
Elevator	....	20	141	20	3	....	....	184
Elevator and switchboard	....	1	21	1	....	....	....	23
Elevator and hallboy	....	....	2	....	....	....	....	2
Firemen.	1	1	10	....	10	2	2	26
Furnacemen	....	....	1	....	1	....	....	2
Gardeners	....	2	2	....	1	....	....	5
Hallmen and doormen	5	26	15	2	1	....	....	49
Housemen.	2	7	11	3	4	1	1	29
Janitors	....	3	4	1	3	2	1	14
Kitchenmen.	6	21	11	3	...	....	....	41
Errand and office boys	1	8	3	....	1	....	....	13
Pantrymen	....	....	1	....	....	....	....	1
Porters.	1	2	9	5	14	10	6	47
Stablemen	4	....	....	....	....	....	....	4
Switchboard	....	7	7	1	1	....	....	16
Usefulmen.	5	31	31	5	1	....	....	74
Waiters	....	22	31	7	6	1	1	68
Total	29	160	324	53	64	24	28	682
Per cent	4.2	23.5	47.5	7.8	9.4	3.5	4.1	100

[1] Day's work, 1 at $1.00 a day, 7 at $1.25 a day, and 15 at $1.50 a day.

TABLE XVIII.—*Concluded.*

FEMALE

Occupations.	Less than $4.00.	$4.00 to $4.99.	$5.00 to $5.99.	$6.00 to $6.99.	$7.00 to $7.99	$8.00 to $8.99.	$9.00 and over.	Total.
Chambermaid	13	56	18	....	2	1	....	90
Chamb. and cook	....	1	3	....	...	....	....	4
Chamb. and laundress	1	6	9	2	....	....	....	18
Chamb. and seamstress	....	....	1	....	....	....	....	1
Chamb. and waitress	32	197	80	....	2	1	....	310
Cleaner	....	....	....	....	2	2	....	4
Cook	....	30	131	38	49	12	7	267
Cook and general housework.	....	2	3	....	....	....	....	5
Cook and laundress.	1	54	104	5	3	....	....	167
Cook and waitress	....	5	3	....	....	....	....	8
Errand girl	1	....	....	....	....	....	....	1
General housework	82	472	399	22	4	....	....	979
Laundress	3	28	23	4	2	....	....	60
Laund and general housework	....	1	....	....	....	....	....	1
Laund. and waitress	....	4	1	1	....	....	....	6
Maid	3	6	3	4	1	....	....	17
Maid (house and parlor)	1	4	2	....	....	1	....	8
Maid (kitchen)	5	13	5	....	....	....	....	23
Maid and seamstress	....	1	....	....	....	....	....	1
Nurse	13	9	2	....	....	....	....	24
Pantry girl.	....	2	1	....	....	....	....	3
Switchboard	....	2	....	....	....	....	....	2
Waitress	10	78	46	2	1	....	....	137
Dishwasher	....	1	....	....	....	....	....	1
Sick nurse	....	....	....	....	....	....	1	1
Total	165	972	834	78	64	17	8	2138
Per cent	7.7	45.5	39.0	3.6	3.0	0.8	0.4	100

The earnings in hotel service play such an important part in the income of males of the Negro group, that some special note was taken of wages for waiters and bellmen. Records of 249 waiters in Manhattan and 46 waiters in Brooklyn showed that they received $25.00 per month, not including tips. Forty-nine bellmen received $15.00 to $20.00 per month, exclusive of tips. Out of these wages lodging and car-fares must usually be paid, and besides uniforms and laundry are not small items of expense.

2. WAGES IN OTHER OCCUPATIONS

The wages of skilled trades do not affect the larger part of the Negro population, because so small a percentage are engaged in these occupations, as reference to the occupational tables in Chapter IV will show. But the numbers are increasing, for there is a constant struggle of Negro wage-earners to rise to these better-paid occupations. Colored carpenters have a local branch of the Amalgamated Carpenters and Joiners Union; there is a street-pavers union, with about a third of the membership Colored men, and the Mechanics Association is composed of Negro artisans of all kinds who wish mutual help in securing and holding work. Since Negroes who are union men are reported to receive the same wages as white workmen, the approximate union wages in 1909 for such skilled occupations as had a considerable number of Negro males will be a good index. The approximate number of Negro union members in 1910 and union wages in 1909 were about as follows: [1] Asphalt pavers and helpers, Negro union members 350, rate of wages, pavers $2.50 per day, helpers $1.75 per day; rock-drillers and tool sharpeners, Negro members 240, employed by the hour, average daily earnings $2.77; cigar-makers, Negro members 165, piece-workers, average daily earnings $2.00; carpenters, Negro members 40, rate of wages $4.50 per day; stationary engineers, Negro members 35, rate of wages, $3.00-$3.50 per day, average weekly earnings, $21.00; bricklayers, Negro members 21, rate of wages $0.70 per hour, average daily earnings $5.60; plasterers, Negro members 19, rate of wages $5.50

---

[1] Bureau of Labor Statistics of New York, *Annual Report*, 1909, pp. 444-595. Figures for Negro members of unions are from Ovington, *op. cit.*, pp. 97-99. Miss Ovington's table seems to show that in 16 occupations the number of Negro members of unions increased from about 1,271 in 1906 to about 1,358 in 1910.

per day; printers (compositors), Negro members 8, average weekly earnings, $24.00; coopers, Negro members 2, average daily earnings $2.50; lathers, Negro members 7, average daily earnings $4.50; sheet-metal workers, Negro members 1, rate of wages $4.50 per day. It is evident that cmpared with the large number of Negro workers few are engaged in the skilled trades, join the unions, and thus enter into the more highly-paid occupations.

3. EFFICIENCY OF WAGE-EARNERS

The efficiency of wage-earners attaches itself to the question of wages. For domestic and personal service, a rich deposit of first-hand material was available in the written testimonials, secured by employment agencies, from the former employers of each applicant seeking work. This is a requirement of the Employment Agencies' Law. The investigator found two employment agencies which had used a printed blank for securing this testimony from former employers of applicants. These blanks asked four questions which are pertinent to the matter of efficiency, and an additional space was left for further remarks. The questions called for answers on the following points: (1) length of time employed, whether applicant was (2) capable, (3) sober or temperate and (4) honest.

In all, 10,095 such blanks were sent out by the agencies during 1906-1909. About 3,000 were returned. Of these about 1,800 replies were excluded from this tabulation because they were received from employers outside of New York, because they were not completely filled out, or were not signed by the parties replying. For this study, 1,182 cases were used. Of these 139 were returned by the Post Office Department as unclaimed, 21 were returned unanswered, while 20 replied that the parties were never in their employ. So there were left 902 complete cases.

These give a fair indication of the whole. The first

point of efficiency is the length of service to one's employer
The records of 100 males do not furnish a sufficient number of cases for any sweeping generalization, yet considerable light is given by the percentages. These show that
30 out of the 100 remained with one employer less than
five months; that 24 remained six to eleven months, and 17
from one year to one year and eleven months, while 25
were in one place for more than two years. Special mention may be made of the five following cases: One of them
remained five years, one seven years, one six years, one
eight years, and one ten or eleven years, with the same employer.

For the females, the percentages will apply well to all
who are wage-earners in domestic and personal service.
Here, also, the largest percentage, 24.1 per cent, remained
in one place from six to eleven months; 21.3 per cent remained three to five months; 16.7 per cent remained one
year to one year and eleven months, and fair percentages
obtain for the longer terms of service: namely, 5.2 per cent
two years to two years and eleven months, and 9 per cent
three years or more. Of those in one place of service for
three or more years, five remained four years; two, four
years and a half; nine, five years; three, six years; four,
seven years; two, eight years; one, twelve years; three,
fifteen years, and one, " eighteen years off and on; " in all,
a total of thirty in 802 cases that were in one place of employment more than three years.

When the shifting life of such a great city and the mobile
character of modern wage-earners, especially in domestic
and personal service, are considered, and when it is remembered that the Negro population because of unusual need
of adjustment to city life feels particularly this unstable
current of influence, this showing of lengthy service for
occupations which have weak tenures of service in all coun-

tries can be interpreted in no other way than favorable for
the reputation of Negro domestic help.

The table, next following, gives the detailed length of
service for the cases covered by the 902 testimonials:

TABLE XIX. SHOWING LENGTH OF SERVICE FOR 902 WAGE-EARNERS IN
SELECTED OCCUPATIONS OF PERSONAL AND DOMESTIC SERVICE,
NEW YORK CITY, 1906–1909.

	Male.		Female.		Total.	
	No.	Per cent	No.	Per cent	No.	Per cent
Under 3 months	19	19	149	18.6	168	18.6
From 3 to 5 months	11	12	171	21.3	182	20.2
From 6 to 11 months	24	24	193	24.1	217	24.1
1 yr. to 1 yr. 11 mos.....	17	17	134	16.7	151	16.7
2 yrs. to 2 yrs. 11 mos....	11	11	42	5.2	53	5.9
3 yrs. and over	14	14	72	9.0	86	9.5
Not stated...............	4	4	41	5.1	45	5.0
Total	100	100.0	802	100.0	902	100.0

The above favorable conclusion, seemingly biased and
against the current opinion, is further borne out by the
other replies as to whether the employee had been capable,
sober or temperate, and honest.

Some allowances should be made in weighing employers
on these last points. Many when asked to speak of former
employees have either probably forgotten points of inefficiency, or do not wish to stand in the way of subsequent
employment, or desire to aid the party in securing such
employment. Sometimes also answers are strong commen-
taries on the hard character of the employers. But when
these things are given due weight there still remains a decided balance in favor of the Negro employee. For, of the
100 males, 27 were certified as very capable; 68 as capable,
4 as fairly so, and only one out of 100 received the con-

demnation, " decidedly no." As to their sober or temperate character, 9 were regarded as excellent, 78 employers said " yes," one replied " fairly so," 11 returned the cautious statement " so far as I know " or " I think so," and one did not answer. As to honesty, they received on the whole good certificates; 12 of the 100 were considered very honest, 81 honest, 4 were placed in the cautionary class, while 3 employers gave no statement on this point.

The testimony for female help shows a tendency as favorable. Taking the percentages which are more significant than the crude numbers, 25.4 per cent were considered very capable, 8.9 per cent very temperate, and 28.2 per cent very honest. 59 per cent of the replies said " Yes " as to their capability, 81.9 per cent said " Yes " as to temperateness and 62.8 per cent gave an affirmative answer on honesty. This makes the decidedly affirmative replies 84.4 out of the hundred capable, 90.8 of the hundred temperate, and 91 out of the hundred honest. Of the employers' testimony, classified as " fairly so," there were 10.5 per cent under capable, 0.1 per cent under " sober or temperate," and 0.4 per cent under honest. Those replying " so far as I know " or " I think so," 0.5 per cent were under capable, 6.5 per cent under sober or temperate, and 7.1 per cent under honest. Those classed under " No " and " Decidedly no " show 2.4 per cent not capable, 0.5 per cent not sober or temperate, and 0.7 per cent not honest. Considering this mass of testimony in whatever light one may, coming as it does entirely from the employers, and applying to that part of the Negro group which probably has the lowest standard of intelligence and economic efficiency and independence, the conclusion is made decidedly trustworthy that Negro wage-earners in domestic and personal service in New York City are capable, sober and honest.

Table XX, following, gives in full the classified replies of employers:

TABLE XX. OPINIONS OF FORMER EMPLOYERS OF 902 NEGRO WAGE-EARNERS IN DOMESTIC AND PERSONAL SERVICE, NEW YORK CITY, 1906–1909.

| | Capable. | | | | | | Sober or temperate. | | | | | | Honest. | | | | | |
| | Male. | | Female. | | Total. | | Male. | | Female. | | Total. | | Male. | | Female. | | Total. | |
	No.	Per cent	No.	Per cent	No.	Per cent	No.	Per cent	No.	Per cent	No.	Per cent	No.	Per cent	No.	Per cent	No.	Per cent
Very	27	27	204	25.4	231	25.6	9	9	71	8.8	80	8.9	12	12	226	28.2	238	26.4
Yes	68	68	473	59	541	60	78	78	657	82	735	81.5	81	81	504	62.9	585	64.9
Fairly so	4	4	84	10.5	88	9.8	1	1	1	1	2	0.2	...	...	3	0.4	3	0.3
"So far as I know," or "I think so."	...	...	4	0.5	4	0.4	11	11	52	6.5	63	7.0	4	4	57	7.1	61	6.8
No	...	...	17	2.1	17	1.9	...	...	4	0.5	4	0.4	...	...	6	0.7	6	0.6
Decidedly no	1	1	2	0.3	3	0.3	...	...	...	...	...	...	...	...	...	...	...	...
Not stated	...	...	18	2.2	18	2.0	1	1	17	2.1	18	2.0	3	3	6	0.7	9	1.0
Total	100	100	802	100	902	100	100	100	802	100	902	100	100	100	802	100	902	100
Total per cent	11.1		88.9		100		11.1		88.9		100		11.1		88.9		100	

These testimonials furnish a body of evidence contrary to the current opinion of criticism and blame, and direct attention to other causes for whatever unsatisfactory part that Negroes are playing in this line of service in the City. These causes may be looked for in the increasing number of European immigrants; in the growing ambition and effort of Negro wage-earners, sharing the feeling of all native-born Americans, to get away from personal and domestic service and to enter fields of work with better wages, shorter hours, and more independence.[1] To this may be added the increasing custom, indicating prejudice of well-to-do Americans, of giving preference to European servants.[2]

The efficiency of Negro skilled workmen is indicated in the replies of 37 employers, summarized in Chapter IV. (See p. *77, supra.*) If they had ever employed Negroes, they were asked whether in comparison with white workmen Negro workmen were:

1. Faster, equal or slower in speed.
2. Better, equal or poorer in quality of work done.
3. More, equally or less reliable.

The consensus of opinion expressed was that the Negro workmen whom they had employed measured up to the white, and there was a general belief that Negroes usually had to be well above the average to secure and hold a place in the skilled trades.

[1] On this point the writer has talked with a number of Negroes who were serving or had served in domestic and personal service. Some of them have gone so far as to enter small business enterprises for themselves. They often remarked: "I want to be my own boss."

[2] From several reliable sources has come testimony concerning employers who formerly had Negro servants, and gave them up for reasons similar to that of one lady who said: "It is going out of fashion to have Colored help any longer." *Cf.* also, Ovington, *op. cit.,* pp. 75-86.

To make a summary of the wages and efficiency: In comparison with the cost of living, Negro men receive very inadequate wages in domestic and personal service except three or four occupations that afford "tips." The small number of skilled artisans who are equal to or above the average white workman and can get into the unions, receive the union wages.

Women for the most part are in the poorly paid employments of domestic and personal service. The small wages of the men and the number of women engaged in gainful occupations (See Chapter IV) show that the women must help earn the daily bread for the family. Their low income power forces these families to the necessity of completing the rent by means of lodgers, deprives children of mothers' care, keeps the standard of living at a minimum, and thus makes the family unable to protect itself from both physical and moral disease.

Although popular opinion may be to the contrary, testimonials signed by former employers show that the large majority of Negroes in domestic and personal service are capable, temperate, and honest, and remain with one employer a reasonable time, considering the shifting condition of city life, the mobility of such wage-earners and the weak tenure of domestic and personal service in a modern city.

PART II

THE NEGRO IN BUSINESS IN NEW YORK CITY

CHAPTER I

The Character of Negro Business Enterprises

I. THE BUSINESS PROMISE

It is a far cry from satisfying an employer to pleasing the public. The one requires the obeying of the orders of a boss, the other calls for initiative and self-direction. Business enterprise involves judgments of the whims, wishes and wants of prospective customers and skill in buying goods or supplying services to satisfy their demands. The wage-earner needs his labor only. The business promoter must secure capital and establish credit. The employee has only the stake of a present place, and has little hindrance from going to another job in case of disappointment. The business man risks name, time, labor and money in the commercial current and has only his experience left, if he loses his venture.

Therefore, the Negro two and a half centuries under the complete control of a master could hardly be expected in one generation to acquire the experience, develop the initiative, accumulate the capital, establish the credit and secure the good-will demanded to-day in carrying on great and extensive business enterprises, such as find their headquarters in New York City, the commercial heart of the continent. Besides, the handicaps of the social environment, due to the prejudices and differences of the white group by which he is surrounded, and to previous condition of servitude, have had their commercial and industrial consequences. Again, speaking for New York City, many of the Negroes who were leaders in whatever business was carried on up to about 1884 were the prominent workers in activities for race liberation and manhood privileges, thus subtracting energy and time from business pursuit. The movement may be likened in a rough way to that of English workingmen before and after about 1848; the first period being a struggle for the liberty of labor and the second period aiming to fill that liberty with manhood and economic content.

This study, then, of what the Negro is doing along business lines in New York City does not show a number of large operations when compared with what goes on in America's greatest commercial Metropolis. But the findings are highly significant for what they disclose of business capacity and possibility. There has been a business development among Negroes in such a competitive community that is both substantial and prophetic.

2. A HISTORY OF THE NEGRO IN BUSINESS

The economic propensity to higgle and barter appeared early among the Negroes of the New Amsterdam Colony. As early as 1684 the Colonial General Assembly passed a law that " no servant or slave, either male or female, shall either give, sell or truck any commodity whatsoever during the term of their service." Any servant or slave who violated the law was to be given corporal punishment at the discretion of two justices and any person trading with such servant or slave should return the commodity and forfeit five pounds for each offense.[1] And further action was taken in 1702 which rendered all bargains or contracts with slaves void and prevented any person from trading in any way with a slave, without the consent of the owner of such slave.[2] The penalty for violation was to forfeit treble the

---

[1] *New York Colonial Laws*, p. 157.   [2] *Ibid.*, pp. 519-21.

value of the commodity and payment of five pounds to the owner of the slave. In 1712, probably after the terror of the Negro riot of that year, it was decreed that no Negro, Indian or mulatto *who should be set free, should hold any land or real estate, but it should be escheated.*[1] The provisions of the two acts of 1684 and 1702 about trading with slaves were revised and re-enacted in 1726.[2]

The character of much of this trade is shown by city regulations which forbade the sale of great quantities of "boiled corn, peaches, pears, apples, and other kinds of fruit." These wares were bought and sold not only in houses and outhouses but in the public streets. The Common Council in 1740 declared the same to be a nuisance and prohibited it with a penalty of public whipping. The Council gave as one of its reasons that it was productive of "many dangerous fevers and other distempers and diseases in the inhabitants in the same city," but those coming to market by order of their masters were excepted from the prohibition. The effect of the latter traffic upon the health of the city was purposely not discerned.[3] The act of 1726 was again re-enacted in 1788.[4] From time to time faithful slaves of the West India Company were set free. These usually began tilling the soil for themselves and probably marketed their products in the town.

Slaves, therefore, had little or no opportunity to share in the trading operations of the Colony. State emancipation by the acts of 1799, 1817, and 1827, however, was finally secured, and with the coming of this boon there was liberty to engage in the traffic of the growing metropolis.

---

[1] Williams, *op. cit.,* vol. i, p. 142.

[2] *New York Colonial Laws,* vol. ii, p. 310.

[3] *Minutes of the Common Council of New York,* vol. iv, pp. 497-98.

[4] *New York State Laws, Eleventh Session,* p. 675.

There is conclusive evidence that considerable numbers of Negroes did embrace the opportunity.

The volumes of the Colored American from 1838 to 1841 contain a number of advertisements and references to business enterprises run by Negroes. The newspaper itself was a considerable undertaking and job printing was also " executed with dispatch." In 1837, George Pell and John Alexander opened a restaurant in the one-hundred block in Church Street.

In 1838, there were two boarding houses in this same block, and two boarding houses in Leonard Street and one each in Spruce and Franklin and Lispenard Streets. The next year two other boarding houses were started, one on South Pearl Street and the other near the beginning of Cross Street, and in 1840 two more entered the list, on Sullivan and Church Streets. The drug store of Dr. Samuel McCune Smith and the cleaning and dyeing establishment of Bennet Johnson, both in the one-hundred block on Broadway, were well known and successful enterprises of the day.

B. Bowen and James Green both had small stores for dry goods and notions in 1838, the former on Walker Street and the latter on Anthony. While the same year a hair-dressing establishment on Leonard Street, a coal-yard on Duane Street, a pleasure garden on Thomas Street and three tailors, whose location could not be ascertained, were enterprises of promise.

In 1839 and 1840, there were a pleasure garden and saloon in Anthony Street and a similar establishment on King Street, with an " Amusement House " on Spring Street, and near it Brown and Wood ran a confectionary and fruit store. Richard Carroll ran a bathing establishment in Church Street. A coal-yard in Pearl Street, a watch and cloak maker, three private schools, and a " dry-goods store of the female Trading Association," complete the list of firms that was contained in the record of the period.

A number of these enterprises are known to have continued for a number of years after 1840. Testimony of witnesses [1] as late as the time of the Civil War shows that a number of the above-named enterprises were in existence as late as 1860.

Also that second-hand clothing shops were frequently run by Negroes, and barber-shops and restaurants of excellent equipment were evidences of activity comparable with the earlier period. Thomas Downing kept a restaurant at the corner of Wall and Broad Streets and from it amassed considerable wealth bequeathed to his children.

In 1869, the Negro caterers had such a large share of this business that the dozen leading ones came together and formed the Corporation of Caterers which was a sort of pool to control the conduct of the business and which was so enlarged after three years under the name of the United Public Waiters Mutual Beneficial Association, that the original purpose was largely sidetracked.[2]

There is little direct evidence available for the period from about 1875 to 1909. The census of 1900 gave a return of Negroes in occupations which may indicate proprietors of establishments, but there is no way of ascertaining whether they owned, operated or were employed in such lines of business. There were in all 488 distributed as follows: Among the males, boarding and lodging-house keepers 10, hotel-keepers 23, restaurant keepers 116, saloon keepers 27, bankers and brokers 5, livery-stable keepers 9, merchants and dealers 162 (retail 155, wholesale 7), un-

---

[1] S. R. Scottron in *Colored American Magazine*, Oct., 1907, and several others interviewed by the writer.

[2] *Vide*, pp. 68-69.

dertakers 15, clock and watchmakers and repairers 2, manufacturers and officials 36, and photographers 22. The females included boarding and lodging-house keepers 50, milliners 9, and photographers 2. A goodly number of Negro enterprises are very probably represented in this list. That this is true is evident from the large number of enterprises in the various lines of business that were found by the canvass of 1909. We may safely infer that the period was one of considerable growth in both the number and variety of business establishments. We shall, therefore, turn our attention to the result of the canvass of the last-named year.

3. THE NATURE OF THE ESTABLISHMENTS IN 1909

The first question which naturally arises is how many Negro business enterprises were in Manhattan in 1909. At the meeting of the National Negro Business League in New York City in 1908, a paper was read on " The Negro Business Interests of Greater New York and Vicinity." This paper gave a total of 565 enterprises. But as this included 100 dressmaking and 14 stenography and type-writing, this estimate doubtless included some cases that upon closer analysis could not have been designated as business establishments.

A Negro business directory of New York City in 1909 gave names and addresses of 567 establishments. Upon investigation some of these could not be found at addresses given. From his own canvass, the writer estimates the number of bona-fide business enterprises in Manhattan to have been about 475. Of this number, records of 332 were secured and the remainder were either visited or certified by reliable testimony. Of the 332 records, 15 have been excluded either because the firm has ceased to do business or the records were too incomplete for use in this monograph; eight of the remainder were corporations and will be treated below separately. This left 309 establishments upon which to base conclusions. These establishments were so distributed as to be fully representative of the whole. According to the kind of service or goods offered to the public, these 309 establishments were as follows:

Barber shops	50
Groceries	36
Restaurants and lunch rooms	26
Tailoring, pressing, etc.	24
Coal, wood and ice	19
Hotel and lodging houses	17
Employment agencies	14
Express and moving vans	12
Undertakers and embalmers	11
Pool and billiard Rooms	10
Dressmaking and millinery	8
Hairdressers	8
Printers	5
Saloons and cafés	5
Miscellaneous	48 [1]
Total	309

Two facts are evident. The largest number of the enterprises are the outgrowth of the domestic and personal service occupations and they are mainly enterprises that call for small amounts of capital.

[1] The 48 miscellaneous establishments were distributed as follows: boot and shoe repairing 6, hand laundries 6, cigar, tobacco and confectionery retailers 5, boot-blacking and hat-cleaning firms 5, fruit and vegetable dealers 4, cigar manufacturers 3, house-cleaning firms 3, garages 2, upholstering and mattress-making establishments 2, watch and jewelry dealers 2, bakeries 2, and bicycle repairer, photographer, hat-cleaner and repairer, hardware and notions, painter and plasterer, tea, coffee and spices retailer, fish retailer and storage firm, one each.

4. OWNERSHIP OF ESTABLISHMENTS

The Negro goes into business mainly as an independent dealer. In the large majority of cases he does not enter into a partnership and even when he does, there are rarely more than two partners. Out of the 309 enterprises in 1909, there were only 49 partnerships and 44 of these were firms of two partners only. There were only three firms with three partners each, one firm with four members and one with five members. To these may be added the eight corporations mentioned above.

Some light is thrown upon the Negro's business enterprises by knowing the birth-place of proprietors, the length of time they had resided in New York City and the occupations in which the proprietors were engaged previously to going into business.

The birth-place of proprietors should be considered in connection with the length of their residence in New York City, because the two facts point to the same conclusion concerning the economic and other stimuli of the environment. So far as birth-place is concerned, the most striking fact is that out of 330 proprietors whose birth-places were ascertained, 220, or 66.66 per cent, were born in Southern states and the District of Columbia, and 65, or 19.7 per cent, in the West Indies. The following Southern states furnished the specified 220 proprietors: Virginia 96, South Carolina 31, Georgia 27, North Carolina 25, Maryland 15, Florida 12, the District of Columbia 5, Delaware 3, Kentucky 2, and Alabama, Arkansas, Mississippi, and Texas 1 each. Besides the Southern and West Indian-born Negro business men, other sections were represented as follows: South America 7, New Jersey 7, New York State 7, Pennsylvania 5, New York City 8, Illinois 2, Bermuda 2, Canada 2, Africa, Indiana, Kansas, Maine, and Massachusetts 1 each.

This proportion of Southern-born proprietors is 0.84 of one per cent less than the proportion of Southern-born in the total Negro population.[1] The 19.7 per cent West Indian is about 10.3 per cent larger than the West Indian proportion in the total Negro population. If the 7 natives of South America be added, the proportion would be 12.4 per cent larger. This condition can hardly be explained on the ground that West Indian Negroes reach New York with more capital, nor is it because West Indians secure employment that is better paid, for they, like the native-born Negroes, are confined to domestic and personal service. It is due both to the better general education of the average West Indian and to the fact that he has been reared in an environment of larger liberty which has developed in him an independence and initiative that respond more readily to the new surroundings. Conversation with numbers of them elicited the information that they had come to this country with the idea of saving money and entering business for themselves.

Facts about the length of residence before January 1st, 1910, of 363 proprietors are no less illuminating than their birth-places. Both show the influence of environment, for we do not find that the majority entered business immediately after taking up their residence in the Metropolis. Exclusive of 50 doubtful and unknown and 11 who were born in New York City, only 11 of the 363 had been in the city less than 2 years, 18 had resided in the city between 2 years and 3 years 11 months, and 33 between 4 years and 5 years eleven months—in all, only 62 had entered business after a residence of less than six years. Of course this is partly due to the time it took to save or secure the necessary capital but that this is not

[1] *Cf.* Part I, Chapter III, pp. 58-59.

the only reason for long residence previous to entering business is shown by the fact that of the 62 who began after less than six years residence, 14 ran barber-shops and 11 had grocery stores, enterprises which require at least a small outlay of capital.

In harmony with this view of the matter the inquiry showed further that 161 proprietors had lived in New York City between 6 years and 9 years 11 months; 108 had been in the city between 10 years and 19 years 11 months; 43 had resided there between 20 years and 29 years 11 months; while 28 had lived in the city 30 years or more.

Considerable weight must then be given to the opinion that is in line with the showing of the West Indian—that Negroes entering business in New York City need to live some time in the atmosphere of such a progressive, liberal community to catch the spirit of its initiative and enterprise.

In support of the conclusion the full table showing length of residence of proprietors of the several classes of enterprises is given (p. 103).

Besides the birth-place of proprietors and the length of their residence in New York City, their occupations previously to their entering upon their present lines of business throw considerable light upon the character of ownership. The natural expectation would be to find connection between the previous occupation of the proprietor and the present business in which he is engaged. In a number of cases this cannot be clearly made out as is the case of 16 brokers and 11 undertakers. Very probably this expectation would not be fulfilled in the cases of many Negroes, because domestic and personal service has been largely the opportunity of employment and the source of savings through which the prospective business venture could be launched. For example, 11 proprietors have been

TABLE XXI. LENGTH OF RESIDENCE IN NEW YORK CITY, BEFORE JANUARY, 1910, OF PROPRIETORS OF 309 NEGRO BUSINESS ENTERPRISES, MANHATTAN, 1909.

Class of establishment.	Length of residence in New York City of proprietors.									Total.
	Less than 2 yrs.	2 yrs.–3 yrs. 11 mos.	4 yrs.–5 yrs. 11 mos.	6 yrs.–9 yrs. 11 mos.	10 yrs.–19 yrs. 11 mos.	20 yrs.–29 yrs. 11 mos.	30 yrs. and over.	Born in New York City.	Doubtful and Unknown.	
Barber shops	1	8	5	8	21	10	4	..	1	58
Brokers	..	..	2	2	8	1	1	2	2	18
Coal, wood and ice	1	1	..	3	6	3	3	1	3	21
Dressmaking and millinery	4	1	..	1	4	..	..	..	1	11
Employment agencies	..	..	1	2	5	4	..	..	5	17
Express and moving vans	..	1	..	..	4	3	3	..	4	15
Groceries	..	2	10	12	15	1	5	..	1	46
Hairdressers, etc.	1	..	..	1	2	1	..	..	4	9
Hotels and lodging houses	..	..	1	2	8	2	1	2	3	19
Pool and billiard rooms	1	..	2	3	2	2	..	..	1	11
Printers	..	..	1	..	2	2	1	1	1	8
Restaurant and lunch rooms	..	3	3	5	5	3	3	2	9	33
Saloons and cafés	1	1	..	..	2	2	..	..	..	6
Tailoring, pressing, etc.	2	..	5	5	8	2	1	1	..	24
Undertakers	..	..	..	1	4	3	..	1	5	14
Miscellaneous	..	1	3	16	12	4	6	1	10	53
Total	11	18	33	61	108	43	28	11	50	363

waiters or waitresses; of these one hotel and lodging-house proprietor, and one restaurant keeper were in enterprises closely connected with their previous occupations; there were three grocers and one coal, wood and ice dealer: enterprises less closely connected. Two pool and billiard-room proprietors, one conductor of a tailoring establishment, one employment agent and one establishment in the miscellaneous class completed the list of those formerly employed as waiters and waitresses. This makes a striking comparison with three hotel and lodging-house keepers and with five restaurant and lunch-room proprietors who formerly were cooks. That many did follow such a natural line of advance from employee to employer is shown in that 80 out of the 309 were previously connected with the same line of business in which they were engaged in 1909 either on a smaller scale or as an employed promoter. A few had tried one line of business before and had changed to that in which they were found. Such was the case with nine who had previously been restaurant keepers, and six who had been in the grocery business. In no case did a proprietor report that he had been an inheritor of independent means or a gentleman of leisure, and had thus found the road which had led him into business.

5. SIZE OF BUSINESS ENTERPRISES

The size of business enterprises was measured in three ways: (1) the number of employees besides proprietors; (2) the floor space occupied and (3) the rental paid for the place in which the business was carried on. Obviously all the enterprises could not be measured by all three tests. For example, the amount of floor space occupied and monthly rental paid by a brokerage firm might not bear so close a relation to size as the number of employees, nor would rental alone be an index of size of a coal, wood and

ice business, since cellars, which call for smaller rental
than other space, are used. But each enterprise was covered
by more than one of the measurements, so that a fair estimate is given of its size.

In ascertaining the number of employees, the attempt
was made to include only those who had no part in the
ownership, but who gave a large part or all of their time
to some work connected with the enterprise. As far as
possible this was confined to paid employees, but in a few
cases the question of wages of those employed could not be
successfully ascertained on account of reticence of the employer. No record was made of whether or not the time of
the proprietor was also put into the business since in this
respect there was great variation among establishments.

Only a small proportion, 77 out of 309 establishments,
were without employees. Yet very few, 21 in all, employed
five or more persons. The largest number, 87, had only
one regular employee, 65 establishments had two employees,
29 had three and 16 had four persons regularly employed.
The number of employees of 14 firms was not ascertained.

Floor space occupied by many establishments is a good
index of size, especially in New York City. Of course, in
the case of such establishments as brokers, employment
agencies and express and moving-van firms that require an
office only, this is not a criterion. But for many other establishments in a city where square feet of floor space is
carefully figured upon in the cost of the product, such a
measure has considerable value in estimating business enterprises. In securing the measurement of floor space in the
different establishments it was not possible to make an
actual measurement in many instances. In some cases the
proprietors knew accurately the length and breadth of the
place they occupied; in other cases where measurements
could not be taken estimates of length and breadth were

made, taking a rough view of the frontage and depth of the building or apartment occupied.

A goodly number of enterprises, such as dressmakers, milliners, shoemakers and tailoring " bushelers " carried on their business in the front room of a ground-floor flat and lived, often with families, in the rear rooms. In those cases, only the floor space of the room used for business purposes was included in the estimate.

Establishments to the number of 17 were estimated as having less than 150 square feet of floor space; six of these were offices of brokers and express and moving-van firms. The greatest number of establishments, 186 in all, were estimated to occupy between 150 and 499 square feet of floor space. Thirty-one establishments occupied between 500 and 999 square feet of floor space; 17 between 1,000 and 1,999 square feet; 4 between 2,000 and 2,999 square feet; 10 between 3,000 and 4,999 square feet; 8 occupied 5,000 or more square feet; 36 were not known—a total of 309 establishments.

Thus, it is seen that the typical Negro business enterprise occupies small floor space, since 234, or 75.7 per cent, of the 309 establishments occupied 999 square feet or less. Table XXII (p. 107) is included to show the details as to floor space in square feet occupied by each class of establishment.

Monthly rental is also a fair indication of the size of a business establishment. In a few cases in which the proprietor said he was owner of the building, a rental was estimated for the portion of the building used for the particular enterprise; in the cases, mentioned above, where the proprietor lived in the rear rooms only a part of the whole rental was estimated as a charge upon the business establishment. So that the figures here given are good measurements of their kind. The facts about 86 establishments

TABLE XXII. ESTIMATED SQUARE FEET OF FLOOR SPACE OF 309 NEGRO BUSINESS ENTERPRISES, MANHATTAN, 1909.

Class of establishment.	Estimated square feet of floor space.								Total.
	Less than 150 sq. ft.	150 sq. ft. to 499 sq. ft.	500 sq. ft. to 999 sq. ft.	1000 sq. ft. to 1999 sq. ft.	2000 sq. ft. to 2999 sq. ft.	3000 sq. ft. to 4999 sq. ft.	5000 sq. ft. and over.	Unknown.	
Barber shops		44	3	2				1	50
Brokers	3	11	2						16
Coal, wood and ice	2	8	3	1				5	19
Dressmaking and millinery		4	2					2	8
Employment agencies	1	10	1					2	14
Express and moving vans	3	4	1					4	12
Groceries	1	29	4	1				1	36
Hairdressing, etc	1	3		1				3	8
Hotels and lodging houses				1	3	6	5	2	17
Pool and billiard rooms		1	1	5		2		1	10
Printers		3	2						5
Restaurants and lunch rooms	1	19	3	1		2			26
Saloons and cafés			1	1			2	1	5
Tailoring, pressing, etc		20	1					3	24
Undertakers		3	4	2				2	11
Miscellaneous	5	27	3	2	1		1	9	48
Total	17	186	31	17	4	10	8	36	309

could not be secured. With the remaining 223, we meet again the evidence of small size of typical establishments, for 180 establishments, or 80.7 per cent, had a monthly rental of $39 or less, and 30 others had a monthly rental between $40 and $79; 16 out of the 223 establishments had a rental of $80 or more per month, and of these 7 paid $150 or more per month.

Judging, then, by the number of employees, by the square feet of floor space occupied and by the monthly rental paid, the typical Negro enterprise is a small retail establishment.

To summarize this chapter: Negroes have had to begin business on a small scale because large capital was lacking and extended experience is yet to be gained. They have, however, even from the days of the Colony, when they were held as slaves, shown a decided propensity for trade, and since state emancipation this has been increased by a desire for economic independence and has expressed itself in enterprises in several lines of business. The variety and number of enterprises have increased with the years. In 1909, Southern born and West Indian Negroes comprised nearly all who had entered business, the latter far in excess of their proportion in the Negro population. This is probably due to initiative developed in an atmosphere freer than that from which the Southern Negro comes. Although confined largely to domestic and personal service occupations, Negroes have had the thrift and initiative to enter many lines of business into which neither the experience nor the capital derived from such employment would be expected to lead. In size, the typical Negro business enterprise has from one to two paid employees, has a floor space of less than one thousand square feet, and pays a rental of between fifteen and forty dollars per month.

CHAPTER II

The Volume of Business

INDICATIONS of the volume of business are in accord with the conclusions from the size of Negro business enterprises. Volume of business was measured (1) by the valuation of tools, fixtures, *etc.,* used in the conduct of the business, (2) by the amount of merchandise kept on hand, if the business was such as required a stock of goods, and (3) by the total gross receipts of the business during the two years, 1907 and 1908.

I. VALUATION OF TOOLS AND FIXTURES

Wood and ice dealers need to invest very little in tools and fixtures. Fourteen out of 19 coal, wood and ice dealers had less than ten dollars so invested. They needed only shovels, baskets and push-carts. The estimated valuation of tools and fixtures of the largest number of establishments fell between $50 and $399; 90 were estimated to be between $50 and $199, and 63 were estimated to be between $200 and $399. Besides these, 37 establishments—1 broker, 5 employment agencies, 1 grocery, 5 hairdressers, 9 restaurants and lunch rooms, 2 "busheling" tailors and 14 miscellaneous had tools and fixtures estimated, with allowance for depreciation, to be worth more than $10 and less than $50. It is important to note, however, that while the numbers with estimated valuation of tools and fixtures between $400 and $1,499 is only 50, those estimated at $1,500 and over number 33.

Judged, then, from the valuation of tools and fixtures,

TABLE XXIII. ESTIMATED VALUATION OF PLANT, TOOLS AND FIXTURES OF 309 NEGRO BUSINESS ENTERPRISES, MANHATTAN, 1909.

Class of establishment.	Estimated valuation of plant, tools and fixtures.										Doubtful and unknown.	Total.
	Less than $50.	$50 to $199.	$200 to $399.	$400 to $599.	$600 to $799.	$800 to $999.	$1,000 to $1,199.	$1,200 to $1,499.	$1,500 to $1,999.	$2,000 and over.		
Barber shops		3	27	8	5	3	1		1		2	50
Brokers	1	5	4				2				4	16
Coal, wood and ice	14										5	19
Dressmaking and millinery		6	1	1								8
Employment agencies	5	5	2	1							1	14
Express and moving vans		1	2	2	1		2			4		12
Groceries	1	22	11	2								36
Hairdressers, etc.	5	2	1									8
Hotels and lodging houses				2	1	1	2		2	7	2	17
Pool and billiard rooms				2			1		4	3		10
Printers		1			1	1				2		5
Restaurant and lunch rooms	9	10	3		1	1				1	1	26
Saloons and cafés								1		3	1	5
Tailoring, pressing, etc.	2	18	2	1							1	24
Undertakers			2	1	1		2		1	4		11
Miscellaneous	14	17	8	3						1	5	48
Total	51	90	63	23	10	6	10	1	8	25	22	309

the magnitude of Negro business enterprises is considerable and falls into three classes: one of comparatively small valuation, 184 estimated below $400; one class of medium valuation, 50 estimated between $400 and $1,499; and one of comparatively large valuation, 33 at $1,500 and over.

The details of these valuations of tools and fixtures are given in full in Table XXIII (p. 110).

2. THE AMOUNT OF MERCHANDISE ON HAND

Next to valuation of tools and fixtures, the amount of merchandise kept in stock is a good index of the magnitude of the business done by many enterprises. Of course, the business of brokers, express and moving-van firms, employment agencies, and some miscellaneous enterprises could not be measured by the amount of stock kept on hand. Also barber shops and pool and billiard rooms sometimes keep a small stock of cigars, tobacco, *etc.* So these firms can not be so measured. The statements about merchandise on hand were accurately estimated either from figures on the books of the firm or from rough inventories of the stock on hand made with the assistance of the proprietor.

Negro business enterprises for the most part are small retail enterprises and do business on the scale of establishments of this type. They have not yet accumulated the capital nor gained the credit to engage in wholesale trade or to carry a stock of merchandise large in quantity or variety such as an extensive patronage demands. But they do handle a considerable amount of business with the small capital they have to invest. When this is compared with the gross receipts for 1907 and 1908 the showing is very creditable.

For, of the 302 enterprises for which estimates of stock on hand were obtained 159 firms, including 46 barbershops and 9 pool and billiard rooms that kept small stocks

TABLE XXIV.—Estimated Valuation of Merchandise on Hand in 241 Negro Business Enterprises, Manhattan, 1909.

Class of establishment.	Less than $50.	$50 to $99.	$100 to $199.	$200 to $399.	$400 to $599.	$600 to $799.	$800 to $999.	$1,000 to $1,999.	$2,000 and above.	Doubtful and unknown.	Refused.	Totals.
Barber shops	14	2	3	1						30		50
Brokers												
Coal, wood and ice	13	2	2	2								19
Dressmaking and millinery			1			1	1			5		8
Employment agencies												
Express and moving vans												
Groceries		1	4	14	8	7	1				1	36
Hairdressers, etc.	3			2						2	1	8
Hotels and lodging houses	1			1				1		14		17
Pool and billiard rooms [1]	3			1						5	1	10
Printers	1							3				5
Restaurants and lunch rooms				1	1							
Saloons and cafés	5	4										5
Tailoring, pressing, etc.		4		3					1	14	4	24
Undertakers				8	1	1	1		2	1		11
Miscellaneous	12	4	4							18		48
Total	52	13	14	33	15	9	3	4	3	62	16	241

1 Cigars and tobacco.

of cigars and tobacco, had a stock of merchandise on hand estimated at less than $50; 20 others ranged between $50 and $99; 38 others had stock on hand in amounts between $100 and $299, while 23 fell between $300 and $599. Thirteen enterprises kept a stock estimated between $600 and $1,000; six ran from $1,000 up, while seven were unknown. In a word, classified by amount of merchandise kept on hand, the firms fell into three classes, the largest class was composed of those having a stock valued at less than $50, the next class grouped those between $50 and $600, and the third and smallest class contained those with stock on hand valued at $600 and above. It will be of help to see in detail how enterprises in each class were grouped according to estimated valuation of merchandise on hand, so Table XXIV showing this is given (p. 112).

3. GROSS RECEIPTS IN 1907 AND 1908

The final and concluding item in measuring the magnitude of Negro business enterprises is the amount of gross receipts of the firms covering a given period of time. For this purpose the years 1907 and 1908 were selected, the first because the greater part of it was before the panic of 1907, the second instead of 1909 because a completed year at the time this canvass was made. A close study of the accompanying table shows that the panic had considerable effect upon the gross receipts of these firms. For example, in 1907, 32 firms had gross receipts less than $1,000; in 1908, 38 firms were in the same group; in 1907, 37 firms did a business of between $1,000 and $1,999; in 1908, 38 firms had the same fortune. And even this does not always show the falling off in gross receipts of the individual firm unless the decrease was sufficient to carry it into a lower group.

Of the total 309 Negro enterprises, 118 were established too recently to have gross receipts in 1907 and 1908, and 63 did not furnish sufficient evidence, so they are classed as doubtful and unknown. This leaves, therefore, 128 enterprises about which sufficient statements of gross receipts were secured to justify discussion. The figures for these, however, were carefully ascertained. For 115 establishments the exact figures were taken from records kept by the firms for the years 1907 and 1908, or the larger part of those years, while the other 13 are estimates based upon careful statements from proprietors and employees of their receipts for months or weeks at different seasons of the two years.

Compared with the general retail lines in New York City the magnitude of Negro business is creditable when judged by gross receipts. Of the 128 establishments, 87 in 1907 and 85 in 1908 handled a gross business of $2,999 or less; 32 firms in 1907 and 38 firms in 1908 had gross receipts between $3,000 and $10,000; and 9 firms in 1907 and 5 firms in 1908 carried on business operations which ranged in gross receipts above $10,000, four of these in 1907 and two in 1908 being $15,000 or more. Considering the amount of merchandise kept on hand and the valuation of tools and fixtures, this business showing indicates that the small amount of capital invested is handled with considerable energy and ability to carry on such an amount of gross business.

It should be noted also that out of 69 establishments in 1907, which had gross receipts less than $2,000, 14 were barber shops, 8 were coal, wood and ice dealers, 4 were employment agencies, 3 were express and moving-vans, 9 were tailors, pressers, *etc.*, and 8 were miscellaneous—a total of 46. And in 1908, out of 76 establishments with gross receipts under $2,000, 18 were barbershops, 8 were ice, coal and wood dealers, 4 were employ-

TABLE XXV. GROSS RECEIPTS FOR 1907 AND 1908 OF 309 NEGRO BUSINESS ENTERPRISES IN MANHATTAN

Class of establishment.	Gross receipts of Negro business enterprises.																Doubtful and unknown.	Established since 1907.	Totals.
	Less than $1,000.		$1,000 to $1,999.		$2,000 to $2,999.		$3,000 to $3,999.		$4,000 to $4,999.		$5,000 to $9,999.		$10,000 to $14,999.		$15,000 above.				
	1907.	1908.	1907.	1908.	1907.	1908.	1907.	1908.	1907.	1908.	1907.	1908.	1907.	1908.	1907.	1908.			
Barber shops	3	5	11	13	7	5	4	2									10	13	50
Brokers	2		4	3	1		1				2	2	1	1			1	5	16
Coal, wood and ice	6	6	2	2				3		1							7	4	19
Dressmaking and millinery	1	1	1	1			1										2	2	8
Employment agencies	1	3	3			1			1			1					8	1	14
Express and moving vans	2	3	2		1		1	2									4	2	12
Printers							1										2	2	5
Groceries	4	3	2	4	3		1	1	1	2	5	6					10	8	36
Hotels and lodging houses			2	2			1	2	1	1	2	2	1	1	1	1	3	10	17
Pool and billiard rooms			2	1		1	3	2									1	8	10
Restaurants and lunch rooms			4	3			1	1										5	26
Tailoring, pressing, etc	5	5	4	5	1	1			1		1	5	3				2	20	24
Saloons and cafes											1	1			1	1	2	13	5
Underta·ers		1	1	1	1	1	1		1			1		1	1	1	2	3	11
Hairdressers	1		1	1	1												2	3	8
Miscellaneous	7	9	3		1	1	1	1		2	1	1	2	1	1		10	24	48
Totals	32	38	37	38	18	9	15	15	5	6	12	17	5	3	4	2	63	118	309

ment agencies, 3 were express and moving-vans, 10 were tailors and pressers, and 9 were miscellaneous—making a total of 52. The majority of the more important classes of business firms such as brokers, barber shops, grocers, printers, hotel and lodging-house keepers, restaurant and lunch-room proprietors, saloon and café firms and undertakers have gross receipts from $2,000 a year and over.

The full showing of classified gross receipts of the 309 establishments is given in Table XXV (p. 115).

Measured, then, by valuation of tools, fixtures, *etc.,* by merchandise on hand, and by gross receipts in 1907 and 1908, Negro enterprises with a small command of capital and credit do a comparatively large gross amount of retail business.

CHAPTER III

Dealing with the Community

THE severest test of a business enterprise is its relation to the community, both the commercial houses with which it deals and the consuming public to whom it sells. With the former a firm must establish credit, with the latter it must build up confidence. Credit is established by the prompt payment of bills, the length of time a firm has been in operation allowing time to make a good reputation and its business methods in dealing with its suppliers. The confidence of customers is secured by the care and accuracy with which orders are filled, the length of time the firm has been in a certain locality and patrons have dealt with it and by the whims and prejudices of the community or locality.

It was out of the question to get data which would cover all of these points, but sufficient material was gathered to throw considerable light on (1) the length of time the firms had been established, (2) the length of time they had been situated at the particular address where they were found, (3) the means used in keeping the accounts of sales, expenditures, *etc.*, (4) whether they gave credit to customers and whether they received credit from suppliers, and (5) what proportion of their customers were white and what proportion were colored.

I. AGE OF ESTABLISHMENTS

Negroes are often said to be able to start but unable to continue in undertakings which require determination, persistence, tact, and which involve strenuous competition. This opinion is certainly not borne out by the age of their business enterprises in New York. For, in the face of conditions they had met in beginning business in New York City, only 51 out of the known 309 enterprises had been established less than one year; 67 between one and two years; 114 between two years and six years, and 33 between six years and ten years. Twenty-two had been established between ten and fifteen years, and twenty were fifteen or more years old, nine of them having been established twenty years or more; the age of two was unknown. When it is remembered that during the first decades after emancipation the larger number of the most energetic Negroes was absorbed in professional occupations, principally teaching, because of the great need in race uplift, and that business pursuits have had until within the last few years minor consideration, to say nothing of trials and failures in the effort to gain business experience, the age of these enterprises must be counted a creditable showing. And it is a good recommendation to the commercial world that the Negro has not made a reputation for bankruptcy assignments. When one reflects that nearly all of these proprietors and promoters have migrated to New York City from less progressive communities and that the chances to get experience in a well-established business before they attempt to start an enterprise for themselves is, except in very rare cases, denied Negroes, the permanency of the ventures in the commercial current deserve commendation.

2. PERMANENCE OF LOCATION

No less interesting than the length of time a firm had been established was the length of time it had been located at the address where it was found by the canvasser in 1909.

TABLE XXVI. SHOWING LENGTH OF TIME 309 BUSINESS ENTERPRISES HAD BEEN AT ADDRESSES WHERE FOUND, MANHATTAN, 1909.

Class of establishment.	Length of time at present address.								Unknown.	Total.
	Less than 6 mos.	6 mos. to 11 mos.	1 yr.–1 yr. 11 mos.	2 yrs.–3 yrs. 11 mos.	4 yrs.–5 yrs. 11 mos.	6 yrs.–7 yrs. 11 mos.	8 yrs.–9 yrs. 11 mos.	10 yrs. and over.		
Barber shops	5	1	13	10	5	3	3	5	5	50
Brokers	1	2	3	2	2	2	1		3	16
Coal, wood and ice	1	2	2	3	1		2	1	7	19
Dressmaking and millinery	1	1	2	3					1	8
Employment agencies		3	2	5	1		1		2	14
Express and moving vans	2	2	1	1	1		1	1	3	12
Groceries	4	6	12	7	4			1	2	36
Hairdressers, etc.	1	1	2	2					2	8
Hotels and lodging houses		2	3	5	1	3		2	1	17
Pool and billiard rooms	1	3	1	2	1			1	1	10
Printers			3	1		1				5
Restaurant and lunch rooms	5	8	3	7	2				1	26
Saloons and cafés		2		2		1				5
Tailoring, pressing, etc.	2	5	10	7						24
Undertakers	1	1		3	1	2	1	1	1	11
Miscellaneous	6	12	13	6	3	2		1	5	48
Total	30	51	70	66	22	14	9	13	34	309

The exact causes which induce the Negro firms to change addresses could not be ascertained, but 81 out of 275 had been at the address where they were found less than one year, although, as shown above, only 51 were less than one year old; 72 had been at their present address between one year and two years, which leaves a smaller margin between that number and the 67 shown to have been established that length of time. There was a similar small margin of comparison in the groupings of two to four and four to six years between the time the firms were established and the length of time they had remained at the one address. This shifting is due probably to the movements of the Negro population upon which the firms depend for patronage, but partly to inexperience.

The first of these facts would have effect on the question of a firm's getting credit on purchases of supplies and both facts mean a great deal in securing and holding a retail trade.

That a detailed comparison may be made, Table XXVI, showing length of time firms had been at addresses where they were found, is added (p. 119).

3. BUSINESS METHODS

The age and permanence of a firm does not influence its success so much as its business methods. And an index of its efficiency in this respect is its methods of accounting. These are shown in the means used for keeping accounts Negro business men were asked whether or not they used ledger, journal, cash-book, day-book, or other records. Some enterprises such as grocery stores, would have need of a mechanical register. If a firm had one, it was inspected. Facts about 49 establishments were not available. Of these, 35 firms had no means of keeping accounts, other than the memories of those running the place. These were,

TABLE XXVII. MEANS FOR KEEPING ACCOUNTS USED BY 309 NEGRO BUSINESS ENTERPRISES, MANHATTAN, 1909.

Means used in accounting by Negro business enterprises.

Class of establishment.	Ledger.		Journal.		Cash-book.		Day-book.		Mechanical cash-register.		Other records.		Un-known.	Totals.
	Yes.	No.	Yes.	No.	Yes.	No.	Yes.	No.	Yes.	No.	Yes.	No.		
Barber shops	2	43	..	45	23	22	7	38	10	35	2	43	5	50
Brokers	13	3	3	13	16	..	8	8	..	16	5	11	..	16
Coal, wood and ice	..	13	1	12	2	11	7	6	..	13	1	12	6	19
Dressmaking and millinery	1	7	..	8	5	3	1	7	..	8	1	7	..	8
Employment agencies	3	11	2	12	10	4	4	10	..	14	14	..	..	14
Express and moving vans	..	10	..	10	4	6	5	5	..	10	1	9	2	12
Groceries	10	25	3	32	12	23	21	14	7	28	2	33	1	36
Hairdressing, etc.	1	4	..	5	1	4	3	2	..	5	5	..	3	8
Hotels and lodging houses	4	6	..	10	3	7	4	6	..	10	2	8	7	17
Pool and billiard rooms	1	9	..	10	5	5	2	8	5	5	..	10	..	10
Printers	2	3	..	5	3	2	..	5	..	5	2	3	..	5
Restaurants and lunch rooms	2	10	..	12	8	4	1	11	..	12	..	12	14	26
Saloons and cafes	3	2	1	4	2	3	2	3	4	1	..	5	..	5
Tailoring, pressing, etc.	2	19	2	19	7	14	8	13	..	21	7	14	3	24
Undertakers	8	3	1	10	5	6	5	6	..	11	11	..	..	11
Miscellaneous	8	32	2	38	16	24	9	31	2	38	11	29	8	48
Total	60	200	15	245	122	138	87	173	28	232	64	196	49	309

however, very small enterprises. Of the 260 remaining, 60, or 23 per cent, kept a ledger, 122, or 46.9 per cent, kept a cash-book, and 33.5 per cent had day-books. Thus showing that 37 more firms kept day-books than kept ledgers, and 62 more firms kept cash-books than ledgers. Of the 260, 28 had mechanical cash registers and 64 had some form of record in addition to or other than those named. In a phrase, the Negro business man is learning the methods of the business world in keeping track of his business affairs, though in most cases they are small. Table XXVII gives the details on this point. (See p. 121.)

4. CREDIT RELATIONSHIPS

The manner and care with which a firm keeps record of the business it transacts is closely connected with its credit relations with the buying and selling community. And both these determine to a large extent its business operations. Considerable light was thrown upon the credit relations of Negro enterprises by finding out, wherever possible, whether a firm gave credit occasionally or habitually to customers and whether it received credit from suppliers. Naturally, many proprietors would not give any reply to such an inquiry, and especially about their credit standing with wholesale firms. On such a delicate point, however, information about the giving of credit was secured from 205 firms, and about the receiving of credit from 94 firms. Of the 205 that furnished statements on the matter of giving credit, 87, or 42.4 per cent, occasionally, and 69, or 33.6 per cent, habitually had given credit to customers, while 49, or 23.9 per cent, did not allow credit. When asked about their credit relations with suppliers, 47 replied that they did receive credit, and 47 that they did not receive any; and 215 gave no reply on this point.

5. THE PURCHASING PUBLIC

Length of time established, length of location at an address, methods of accounting and the credit relations play no more important a part in the efforts of Negroes to build up their business enterprises than do the subtle whims and prejudices of the community. This is shown first by the location of nearly all the enterprises in Negro neighborhoods. Of all the 309 enterprises, 288 were located either within or upon the border of the Negro districts. It may be expected, of course, that Negroes will look to their own people first for their patronage, but they should be allowed to cater to the public at large, especially in a cosmopolitan commercial center like New York. In the case of real estate brokers, this is partly true and has grown partly out of the Negro broker's ability to handle more successfully than others properties tenanted by Negroes. It is not generally the case in other lines of business, however, as the testimony of many Negro business men shows.

It was difficult to get statements that would be a basis for a percentage estimate of how liberally white people traded with these Negro firms. Brokers gave no statements that could be so used because nearly all of the 16 brokers had many transaction which involved white owners and colored tenants, white or colored sellers and white or colored buyers. Employment agencies faced a similar situation. Of the other 279 firms, 81, or 29.7 per cent, reported no white customers; 92, or 33.3 per cent, reported that less than 10 per cent of their customers were white. Thus 63 per cent of the Negro business firms have to depend upon the small purchasing power of their own people for the trade with which to build up their enterprises. This is partly due to the feeling of the Negroes in business that they are to cater mainly to Negroes and partly to their inexperienced way of handling customers. But the main reasons are the difficulties they have in renting places in desirable localities and in the refusal of white people to patronize Negroes in many lines of trade.[1] Of the remaining firms 42, or 15 per cent, reported between 10 and 49 per cent white customers. The numbers above were small and only one firm, in the class of dressmaking and millinery, and three in the miscellaneous class, reported an exclusive white trade.

What a battle the Negro business man has to fight can be surmised when to the fact of a narrow patronage from his own people, who have the small purchasing power of their low-paid occupations, is added the severe competition of white firms with larger capital, with more extended credit and larger business experience, that vie with him for even this limited field. Table XXVIII (p. 125), which follows, was compiled on the basis of proprietors' statements of the probable number of white and colored customers over a given number of months. It is about as accurate as such an estimate can be and is far more reliable and definite than general impressions. The percentages of white customers are given, it being understood that the remainder were Negroes. This small amount of information is very significant in showing how the attitude of the white public affects the economic advancement of the Negroes.

In the foregoing chapter we have reviewed some very definite facts concerning the Negro business man's dealing with the community. We have seen that his enterprises are permanently established although against great odds,

---

[1] This conclusion is based upon the statements of Negroes that white people have entered their stores apparently to buy, but beat a retreat upon finding a Negro in charge. Two Negro proprietors employed white workmen to call at residences, etc., in the operation of their businesses while they kept in the background. The writer traced out cases of refusals to rent places to Negro firms. Some of the incidents would be amusing if they were not tragic.

TABLE XXVIII. ESTIMATED PROPORTIONS OF WHITE CUSTOMERS OF 279 NEGRO BUSINESS ENTERPRISES, MANHATTAN, 1909.

Class of establishment.	None.	Estimated Proportion of Whites of Total Customers of Negro Business Enterprises.							Doubtful and Unknown.	Total.
		Less than 10%.	10%–24%.	25%–49%.	50%–74%.	75%–89%.	90%–100%.	100%.		
Barber shops	16	23	7	2					2	50
Brokers										
Coal, wood and ice	5	5	3	1			2		3	19
Dressmaking and millinery	1	1			2	2	1	1		8
Employment agencies										
Express and moving vans		1	1	1	6		2		1	12
Groceries	10	18	2	4		2				36
Hairdressers, etc.	1	5		1	1					8
Hotels and lodging houses	15	1			1					17
Pool and billiard rooms	3	3	2	2						10
Printers				2	3					5
Restaurant and lunch rooms	16	7	1		2					26
Saloons and cafés	1	1				1	2			5
Tailoring, pressing, etc.	4	9	2	5	2	1	1			24
Undertakers	5	6								11
Miscellaneous	4	12	4	2	11	4	6	3	2	48
Totals	81	92	22	20	28	10	14	4	8	279

but that permanence of address is not so well secured. Nearly all, 260 out of 309, were known to have some of the usual methods of keeping accounts, and of the 205 from whom information on the matter was obtained about three-fourths gave credit either occasionally or habitually; while of the 94 who answered as to their receiving credit, about half did and the other half did not receive credit.

The attitude of the white purchasing public has had a tremendous effect on Negro business, because it has failed to forget color in its business dealings. In many lines of business white people will not patronize Negroes at all and about two-thirds of all enterprises depend upon the low purchasing power of the Negro group. The idea that white people will not trade with them to any considerable extent and that they must depend upon their own people is so steeped into the mind of the Negro that he often does not perceive that he is catering to the whole public, white and black.

CHAPTER IV

Some Sample Enterprises

In the first chapters on Negro business enterprises, the several classes of establishments were described in order to present a picture of business among Negroes as a whole. A more concrete idea of the organization and operation of these enterprises, as well as of the proprietors who own and operate them, may be gained from detailed descriptions of selected establishments of each kind. These have been chosen as representing a fair type of the classes to which they belong. On some points there may be wide variations, but each class as a whole is fairly represented by those detailed.

I. INDIVIDUALS AND PARTNERSHIPS

Establishment No. 1 was a barber shop started in 1898, and moved once to the present address eleven years before. The proprietor was born in Savannah, Georgia, had resided in New York City for about twenty years, and was a journeyman barber before starting his own shop. He employed four barbers besides himself, paying each barber between forty and fifty per cent of his receipts. This shop was about 12 feet by 40 feet, and the rental was $30.00 per month. The estimated value of his tools and fixtures was about $700.00, and the estimated gross receipts of his business were $3,500.00 in 1907 and $4,000.00 in 1908. The proprietor kept a cash-book which he balanced once a week. He started his enterprise with one chair, bought with savings from his earnings as a barber. He did a strictly cash

business. His customers were Negroes only, although he
kept a first-class, cleanly place, was in a district where
there were a large number of small white business establishments and some white tenants, and bought his supplies from a white firm.

No. 2. This was a barber shop established in 1890, had
moved twice, and had been located at the last address four
years. The proprietor called himself " the pioneer " as he
visited New York City in 1856-7 and had been living here
32 years in 1909, coming from Calvert County, Maryland.
He had worked as a barber in a shop run for white customers, and by this means saved money to set up for himself in Mott Haven some years before opening in New
York. He employed one additional barber, had a shop
about 12 feet by 28 feet, for which he was paying $35.00
rent. His tools and fixtures were worth about $200.00,
and his gross receipts amounted to about $900.00 in 1907
and about $850.00 in 1908. He used a cash-book and oc-
casionally credited customers, although he paid cash for
supplies from a white firm. His shop was located in a distinctly Negro neighborhood and all his customers were
Negroes.

No. 3. This establishment was a grocery store started
by a West Indian at the address where it was found, who
took a partner at the beginning of the second year. The
junior partner, a Virginian by birth, was brought to New
York by his mother 12 years previously, while the other
had resided here ten years. The senior partner had a very
small grocery business during one year in the West Indies
and worked as an elevator boy and saved capital after coming to New York, as his change of residence had absorbed
his limited resources. The Virginian was peddling tea and
coffee before entering the firm. He had been a porter
in a department store, but preferred " to be independent,

as it seemed too hard to work for another man." They employed one helper and both put in their time; they occupied a floor space 20 feet by 40 feet, at a rental of $35.00 per month. The tools and fixtures were estimated at $350.00; these included a safe and a large national cash register. The careful inventory of stock showed $450.00 worth on hand, and the gross receipts from May, 1908, to May, 1909, was estimated at $6,000.00. The large national cash register and bank book were sufficient means of keeping accounts for the strictly cash conduct of the business. Only a few whites, about all of whom were Jews, live in the blocks adjoining the Negro neighborhood. They found this store most convenient and traded with the firm, but more than five-sixths of its customers were Negroes. The firm sent out hand-bills weekly, and used other forms of advertisement.

No. 4 was a grocery, started in September, 1906, at the same address where it was found by the investigator. The proprietor came from the West Indies to New York City about 12 years previously and engaged in hotel work by means of which he saved his capital. He was still so employed, while his brother conducted the store. The store room was about 14 feet by 40 feet, at a rental of $35.00 per month. The tools and fixtures were valued at $100.00, and the merchandise on hand at about $300.00. The estimated gross receipts were between $2,500 and $3,000 in 1907, and about $2,700 in 1908. Only a cash-book was used in keeping accounts. This was balanced once a week, and an inventory of the stock was taken once a quarter. Credit was habitually allowed to customers, all of whom were Negroes. No whites lived in the neighborhood.

No. 5. This was a real-estate and insurance agent, who began business in July, 1907, and had moved once since. He was born in Virginia and had been in New York City twelve years. This man's business career started as soon as he left college, as his father had given him an education and arranged affairs to that end. He entered his father's barber shop in Virginia and remained three years, then came to New York and started a club and saloon business with capital brought from his native home. This was carried on four years and sold out. After several intervening years, the present enterprise was started on some of the capital derived from the sale of the previous establishment. He employed two collectors, had an office space of about 12 by 40 feet in one of the tenements of which he had charge. His gross receipts from commissions, *etc.,* were about $2,300.00 in 1908. Ledger, cash-book and day-book were used in accounting. The landlords of the properties he handled were all white, but all tenants were Negroes. The real estate sales and exchanges he has handled have been of a similar kind.

No. 6. This was a real estate broker who began business in November, 1903, in Nassau street and moved to his present address two years later. He was born in New York and has always made his home there. Before he finished his high school course, he worked during spare hours and vacations for a real estate firm. After graduation from high school, he started to work with the same firm on a commission basis until he began business for himself as a regular broker. He employed two assistants in his business and had an office in one of the large buildings in the Wall Street district. His office was modestly but adequately furnished, the fixtures, typewriter, *etc.,* estimated at $200.00. In 1907 his gross receipts from commissions, fees, *etc.,* were over $2,500, and in 1908 over $3,000. His capital was accumulated from the business; he used ledger and cash-book in his accounting and both gave and received credit in his transactions. He was a member of the New York Fire Insurance Exchange, and has done considerable study in evening courses on insurance, banking, *etc.* About 95 per cent of his business dealings were with white people.

No. 7. This enterprise in dressmaking and ladies tailoring was started in August, 1906, at the address where found. The proprietress came from her native city, Pittsburgh, Pa., to New York three years previously, and set up her establishment with money she had saved from sewing in Pittsburgh. She employed three helpers and used for business purposes the front room of her apartment, which rented for $25.00 per month. Her tools and fixtures were valued at about $175.00, and she kept less than $100.00 worth of stock on hand, as all work was to order. Gross receipts were about $2,300 in 1907, and about $3,000 in 1908. A cash-book only was used in keeping accounts. About three-fourths of the customers were white.

No. 8. This is an employment agency started about 1889 by the proprietor who came from Delaware the year preceding. In the flourishing days when Negro help was in large demand he made money and formerly employed two or three helpers. When seen, he alone did not find full employment. His fixtures were worth less than $50. He used two front rooms of his living apartment for business purposes. His gross receipts in 1907 were $1,316, and in 1908, $1,076. He used a cash-book and the two record books required by the employment license law. He supplied colored help for white families almost entirely; business was running low because white help was " displacing the colored help of years past."

No. 9. This was a restaurant, established in September, 1904, and moved to the present address two years later. The proprietor was born in Jacksonville, Florida, and had resided in New York six years when interviewed. He was a cook and head-waiter before beginning business for himself. He had two employees, his place occupied a 14 feet by 40 feet basement, for which he paid about $18.00 rental. His fixtures, *etc.*, were valued at about $150, and his gross receipts were about $3,500 in 1907, and $3,000 in 1908. He had saved money for the enterprise while engaged in hotel service in Jacksonville. All his customers were Negroes, except one white regular customer. He admitted occasionally giving credit to customers, although a sign on the wall said, " Positively, no trust."

No. 10. This firm sold coal, wood and ice. It was established in September, 1907, at the address where found, by a native Virginian who had lived in New York seventeen years, and had previously worked as a porter in a jewelry house. No help was employed and the small amount of stock on hand, between $40 and $50, was kept in a cellar about 12 feet by 18 feet. For this a rental of about $8.00 per month was paid. The gross receipts amounted to about $800 in 1908. The proprietor had saved some money from his previous occupation on which to begin; he was located in a Negro neighborhood, so depended entirely on their patronage. He habitually gave credit to customers but received none from his white suppliers.

No. 11. This tailoring establishment was started in September, 1907, by a West Indian, who had lived in New York eighteen years and had worked as journeyman tailor in St. Christopher, W. I. He had moved five times since the business was begun. He did mostly cutting and fitting, but some " busheling." He did not employ any help, and lived in two rooms in the rear of his business place, paying $25 per month for all. The tools and fixtures were worth about $150, and the stock on hand about $50, while gross receipts had amounted to $1,200 in 1907 and about $1,100 in 1908. He kept a cash-book; gave credit occasionally, but received none.

This proprietor said he came to New York leaving paying work behind, because of tales of high wages in his trade; that at first he answered advertisements for journeymen but was turned away when they saw he was a Negro. Finally, he worked as waiter to get money to start for himself. His first " stand " was in a white neighborhood with white trade, but when a considerable number of Negro customers began to frequent his place the neighbors made objections to the landlord, who would no longer rent him the place. At the time of the interview he was in a Negro neighborhood and had only four or five white customers.

No. 12. This also was a tailoring firm, started in 1907, which did mainly cleaning, pressing and repairing ("busheling"). The proprietor was a Georgian by birth, came to New York six years previously, and worked as a valet, and as elevator man in an apartment. He employed one part-time assistant, used for his business the front room, about 12 feet by 14 feet, of an apartment which rented for $25 per month. His tools and fixtures were valued at $140, and he carried about $75 worth of second-hand clothing in stock. His gross receipts in 1908 were about $800. He kept lists of work done for customers. He had been in the same line of business for seven years in his native state, and both times had saved wages to carry out his " desire from a lad up to do business." About two-thirds of his customers were white, and he gave credit habitually.

No. 13. This firm for express and moving service was established in September, 1902, in the same block where found, by a Virginian, who had lived in New York City fifteen years and who worked as a Pullman porter before beginning in this line of business. He usually employed from five to seven men, according to the seasonal trade. He had an express wagon and two vans, which with the horses were valued at $1,200. His gross receipts amounted to about $3,100 in 1907, and about $3,600 in 1908. In keeping accounts both ledger and day-book were used. The proprietor had run a small grocery in Virginia before coming to New York, and some of the capital from its sale had been saved and put into this enterprise. He depended upon white customers for about two-thirds of his patronage.

No. 14 was a manicurist and hair-dressing firm started by the proprietress in May, 1903, who had been in New York eleven years in 1909 and who worked at a pocket-book factory before starting into this venture. She was a native of Virginia. The enterprise was not large enough for any employees; tools and fixtures were worth about $60, and hair goods, *etc.,* on hand were valued at $75; the front room, about 12 by 14 feet, of the living apartment was used for business purposes. In 1907 and 1908 the gross receipts averaged about $1,000, which was mainly fees for manicure and hair-dressing services. This enterprise was started that the proprietress might " be at home," and a cash trade almost solely among white people was being developed.

No. 15. This was an undertakers establishment started in 1897 by a minister, who came to New York from Virginia about twenty-five years ago. The firm had been located at the address where found about nine years, and had a branch in another part of Manhattan. Two helpers were employed, the floor space was about 20 by 40 feet, for which a rental of $35 per month was paid. Tools and fixtures, including dead-wagon, were valued at $1,200, and about $300 of stock was kept on hand. The gross receipts of the business were about $9,000 in 1907, and about $8,000 in 1908. Ledger, cash-book, day-book, and funeral register were used in keeping accounts. The proprietor started on a small saving from his salary as a minister, having to run the business a year before he had the additional $200 in cash for deposit for registration in the Casket Makers Association, thus securing credit on supplies. He habitually allows credit to customers, all of whom, with very rare exceptions, are Negroes.

No. 16 was a hotel on the European plan, established in 1899 by a Georgian who had been in New York five years previously and had saved his wages in several kinds of hotel work to get his start. He usually employed six helpers; the place occupied a four-floor building about 25 by 60 feet, for which a rental of $1,800 per year is paid. Fixtures, furniture, *etc.*, were valued at $2,000. The gross receipts of the hotel were a little over $10,000 in 1907, and between $9,000 and $10,000 in 1908. Both ledger and cash-book were used in keeping accounts. Nearly all customers were Negroes, and whites were not especially sought because those who did come were usually looking for a colored dive and did not act in an orderly way. Credit was occasionally allowed customers and the firm had such standing that it could get such amounts from suppliers as it wished.

No. 17 was a pool-room with a club arrangement in connection. It was started in 1901 by a native of Virginia, who had been living in New York eleven years. The firm had moved once since its establishment. The proprietor was a waiter before beginning this enterprise; he employed two helpers, his place occupied three floors about 25 by 40 feet, and he paid a rental of $75 per month. His fixtures, tables, *etc.*, were valued at between $1,800 and $2,000, and he said they were all paid for. In 1907 the gross receipts were about $3,400, and in 1908 about $3,700, the " best year." A cash-book was kept and balanced twice a year. Negroes " almost altogether " were customers. This proprietor had an ambition from boyhood to run a business and at one time had a second-hand furniture store in Long Branch, N. J.

No. 18 was a job-printing house, started in June, 1908, run since that time at the same place by two partners, one of whom was born in Washington, D. C., the other in the West Indies. The West Indian had been in New York fifteen years in 1909, and had been in the same business once before; the other had been in New York twenty-five years; both had saved money as they worked as journeymen printers before entering business for themselves. At the time of the interview they did not employ any helpers, but their tools, fixtures, *etc.,* were valued at about $900, and the floor space occupied was about 14 by 25 feet. The gross receipts during the six months of 1908 were about $900, and the monthly average for the first month of 1909 was somewhat higher. A cash-book was used in keeping accounts, and about one-third of their customers were white people. They did a strictly cash business.

No. 19 was a saloon and café which was opened in November, 1908, at the place where found. The proprietor came from Kentucky to New York about ten years previously and worked in a cigar store. He employed from seven to nine helpers, and his place occupied about 20 by 60 feet floor space, with a rathskeller in the basement; he paid $100 per month rental. Fixtures, *etc.,* were valued at about $2,200, and stock was kept on hand to the amount of between $700 and $800. Sufficient data for an estimate of gross receipts were not forthcoming. Ledger and cash-book, with cash-register, kept record of business transacted. Customers were " Negroes, almost exclusively " with a " white person now and then." At one time the proprietor ran a cigar store, growing out of his work in such an establishment.

2. THE NEGRO CORPORATION

As was pointed out in a previous chapter, the Negro enters business either alone or with one or two partners. Small enterprises can be so financed. But for undertakings that require considerable capital those who enter them must either have large means or a number must combine their small funds.

The Negro is alert to business lines which offer chances of profit. He is slowly learning the method of " big business." The corporation, with its advantages of impersonal responsibility, facility for taking in or releasing members, and particularly its combined capital, has been adopted in a few cases. These can be treated briefly for what variations they show from the general type.

One of these was a corporation that ran a garage, furnished storage and other care for machines and operated a line of taxicabs, employing from nine to eleven men. Three of the firm members had been employed chauffeurs and thus got the idea and the money to start the firm. There was storage space for about 50 cars. One of the proprietors came from Georgia, another from North Carolina. They had a book-keeper and the usual books for a business house. Five Negro owners and about forty white owners were storing cars with them.

Another enterprise was a corporation of undertakers with a board of eight directors, who held nearly all of the stock. In size they had four employees, occupied a floor space of about 1,200 square feet at a monthly rental of $150. The investments represented about $1,500 in dead-wagon and fixtures and a stock on hand of about $1,000. The gross business was between $9,000 and $10,000 in 1907, the first year of the business; and over $20,000 in 1908. At its organization there were ten corporators who subscribed about $300 each to float the enterprise. It is interesting to note that a hotel-keeper, a minister, three men in other lines of business and the manager of the concern were among these ten.

Two other corporations were printing establishments, each with six original incorporators. One firm did job printing. The other was a publisher of popular songs and has produced several of New York's most popular airs. They had two and ten employees, occupied about 158 and 3,000 square feet of floor space, respectively. The larger firm had a plant valued at between $4,000 and $5,000, kept several hundred dollars worth of stock on hand and did a gross business of about $15,000 in 1907, and about $17,000 in 1908. The smaller firm had been organized in 1909. The larger had run more than four years. The corporators of the smaller concern included an editor, a messenger, silk-factory employee, and laundry employee; those of the larger, a liquor dealer, two actors and three composers of popular songs.

The four other corporations were real estate firms, a line of business requiring considerable capital and attracting the higher grade of business ability. In these instances, all except one firm was composed of the few original incorporators, making the arrangement only a little removed from a partnership. The one exception was a large concern with a capital stock of over $500,000. The previous occupations of the principal promoters of this company included a lawyer, a pharmacist and two real estate brokers.

The stock of this concern was held by small investors in many parts of the United States. The firm at one time employed over 200 people in and out of New York, and claimed to have done an annual business of over $200,000. At some period in its history it may have done so large a business, but this was probably only for an exceptionally prosperous year. This may have led to too sanguine attempts on the part of the promoters. Because of other poor business methods and bad attempts at investment the enterprise failed in the winter of 1910-11.

Three obvious points are shown by the facts concerning these corporations: First, they were composed of only a few members and therefore were not far removed from large partnerships. This set a large limit to command of capital for there were no large capitalists in New York among Negroes. Second, this form of combining capital and business ability has been tried in a few lines of business only—three in all, if we exclude the garage. Third, as seen in their previous occupations, the promoters were men above the average in ability and of some experience.

CONCLUSION

CONCLUSION

THE significance of the foregoing facts is clearly indicated by the summaries following each set of figures. The road to the conclusions is straight. Turning to the preceding chapters, let us see what conclusions are warranted.

The urban concentration of the Negro is taking place in about the same way as that of the white population. In proportions, it varies only to a small extent from the movement of the whites, save where the conditions and influences are exceptional. The constant general causes influencing the Negro population have been similar to those moving other parts of the population to cities. The divorce from the soil in the sudden breaking down of the plantation régime just after the Civil War and the growth of industrial centers in the South, and the call of higher wages in the North, have been unusually strong influences to concentrate the Negro in the cities. It is with him largely as with other wage-earners: the desire for higher wages and the thought of larger liberty, especially in the North, together with a restlessness under hum-drum, hard rural conditions and a response to the attractions of the city, have had considerable force in bringing him to urban centers. Labor legislation in the South has played its part in the movement.

The growth of the industrial and commercial centers of the South, the larger wages in domestic and personal service in the North, and social and individual causes of concentration bid fair to continue for an indefinite period.

The Negro responding to their influence will continue to come in comparatively large numbers to town to stay.

But the Negro's residence in the city offers problems of maladjustment. Although these problems are similar to those of other rural populations that become urban dwellers, it is made more acute because he has greater handicaps due to his previous condition of servitude and to the prejudiced opposition of the white world that surrounds him. His health, intelligence and morals respond to treatment similar to that of other denizens of the city, if only impartial treatment can be secured. Doubtless death-rate and crime-rate have been and are greater than the corresponding rates for the white populations of the same localities, but both crime and disease are a reflection of the urban environment and are solvable by methods similar to those used to remedy such conditions among white people, if prejudiced presuppositions, which conclude without experiment or inquiry that Negroes have innately bad tendencies, give place to open-minded trial and unbiased reason. Snap-shot opinions should be avoided in such serious questions and statesmen, philanthropists and race leaders should study the facts carefully and act accordingly.

The study of the wage-earners among the Negroes of New York City has disclosed conditions and led to conclusions in line with the foregoing inferences. The Negro population was solidly segregated into a few assembly districts, thereby confining the respectable to the same neighborhoods with the disreputable. This population is made up mainly of young persons and adults of the working period of life, attracted to the city largely from the South and the West Indies, principally by the thought of better industrial and commercial advantages. Single persons predominate and the percentage of the aged is low. High rents and low incomes force lodgers into the families to disturb normal home life.

From the early days of the Dutch Colony the Negro has had a part in the laboring life of this community. While most of the wage-earners have been engaged in domestic and personal service occupations, figures that are available warrant the inference that the Negro is slowly but surely overcoming the handicaps of inefficiency and race prejudice, and is widening the scope of employment year by year. What the individual asks and should have from the white community is a fair chance to work, and wages based upon his efficiency and not upon the social whims and prejudices of fellow-workmen, of employers, or of the community.

In domestic and personal service the Negro is poorly paid compared with the cost of living. And even in skilled occupations, where unions admit him and wages are offered equal to those of white workmen, the Negro must be above the average in speed, in quality of work done, and in reliability to secure and hold places.

In domestic and personal service, the verdict from a large body of evidence is that, judged by the testimony of employers as to the length of time employed, the capability, sobriety and honesty of the workers, Negroes furnish a reliable supply of employees that need only to be properly appraised to be appreciated. What is needed for the workers in this class of occupations and for those in the skilled trades, is that more attention be given to adequate training, that more facilities be offered and that a more sympathetic attitude be shown them in their efforts for better pay and better positions.

In reviewing the Negro's business operations judgment should be tempered by consideration of his past and of the tremendous odds of the present. There are handicaps due to the denial of the chances of getting experience, to inefficiency born of resulting inexperience, to the difficulty of securing capital and building credit and to the low purchasing power of the patronage to which a prejudiced public limits him. He is not only denied experience, sorely limited in capital and curtailed in credit, but his opportunities for securing either are very meagre. In spite of all this, there has been progress which is prophetic of the future.

From the days of slavery Negroes have tried the fortunes of the market place and under freedom their enterprises have increased in number and variety. At the present time Southern-born and West Indian Negroes form the bulk of the business men, the latter far in excess of their proportion in the Negro population. This success of West Indians is partly a result of training and initiative developed in a more favorable environment, as they had the benefit of whatever opportunities their West Indian surroundings offered.

Although they gained the meagre capital chiefly from domestic and personal service occupations, Negroes have entered and maintained a foothold in a number of lines of business unrelated to these previous occupations. One of the most important findings is that Negroes form few partnerships and that those formed are rarely of more than two persons. Co-operative or corporate business enterprises are the exceptions. This fact has its most telling effect in preventing accumulations of capital for large undertakings. But co-operation in business is largely a matter of ability born of experience and where can Negroes get this experience in well-organized firms, under experienced supervision? For it is more than a matter of school instruction in book-keeping and the like. In practically the entire metropolis, they rarely get beyond the position of porter, or some similar job. Some fair-minded white people who wish to help the Negro help himself could do great service for the economic advancement of the Negro by throwing open the doors of business positions to a number of ambitious, capable Negro youths, who would thus enter the avenues of economic independence. The writer knows of three Negroes in New York City who proved themselves so efficient in their respective lines that they were taken in as members of large firms.

Another serious matter is connected with this point. All 309 firms were retail establishments, all of them bought from wholesale suppliers who so far as could be ascertained were white firms. In some lines, there were sufficient retailers to support a wholesale house if their purchases were combined. For example, the group of 50 barber shops or of 36 grocers would each support a jobber if they pooled their patronage. But this would demand an organizing power, a business initiative, a fund of capital and a stretch of credit, which only some men experienced in the method of the modern business world could possess.

The small size and scope of Negro enterprises cannot be attributed to lack of business capacity alone. For the gross receipts of the selected years taken in connection with the valuation of tools and fixtures, and with the stock of merchandise on hand showed considerable diligence and thrift in turning these small resources to active use.

The variety of the many small establishments indicates also the initiative of the Negro in using every available opportunity for economic independence. As we have seen, some of the proprietors had early ambitions for business careers, and others had worked hard and saved carefully from small wages that they might rise from the class of the employed to that of employers. The public to which the Negro business man caters should accept his wares and his services for their face value and not discount them because of the complexion of his face.   Then, too, Negroes must learn that the purchasing public desires to be pleased and is larger than the limits of their own people.

Negro wage-earners and business men have great difficulty in scaling the walls of inefficiency and of race prejudice in order to escape the discomforts and dangers of a low standard of living.

FAMILY SCHEDULE

Serial No.	Surname:
Date:	Address:
Investigator.	Floor: No. of rooms: Bath? Rent:
Source of information.	Location on floor: front, rear, right, left.

FAMILY SCHEDULE.

No. in family:
No. earning wages:
No. depending on family income:

EDUCATION AND INDUSTRIAL TRAINING. *

Family Members.	Age.	Place of Birth.	Time. in N. Y.	Reason for coming to N. Y.	MARITAL CONDITION						Chr. +	Pol. ×	Read.	Write.	Mos. in School.	Mos. in College.	Mos. in Industrial sch.	Mos. at Trade.	Trade.	Where followed.
					Mar.	Sing.	Wid.	Div.	Sep.											
1. Man.																				
2. Woman.																				
(Sex.)																				
3.																				
4.																				
5.																				
6. (Lodgers)																				
7.																				
8.																				

* OCCUPATION. (State exact kind of work done and weekly pay.)

Family Members.	At present time.	Weekly Pay.	Hours per day.	During past year.	Weekly Pay.	Days lost past year.	During entire time in New York City.
1. Man.							
2. Woman.							
(Sex.)							
3.							
4.							
5.							
6. (Lodgers)							
7.							
8.							

+ Church affiliations.
B=Baptist.
M=Methodist.
E=Episcopal.
P=Presbyterian.
C=Catholic.
MN=Moravian.

× Political affiliations.
R=Republican.
D=Democrat.
S=Socialist.
PB=Prohibition.

* See space for remarks on other side (3) (4).

FAMILY SCHEDULE (REVERSE SIDE)

Family Members.	UNSUCCESSFUL APPLICATIONS FOR WORK.* (1)			REASON FOR REFUSAL.* (1)				TRADE UNION, SECRET SOCIETIES.* (2)	
	Date.	Place: Name and Address.	Kind of Work.	Place Filled.	Lack of Skill.	Color.	Other.	Name of Organization.	Why not member? Did you apply?
1. Man...									
2. Woman...									
(Sex.)									
3.........									
4.........									
5.........									
6.(Lodgers)									
7.........									
8.........									

*(1) Remarks on Unsuccessful Applications:

*(2) Remarks on Trade Unions and Secret Societies:

*(3) Remarks on Occupation:

*(4) Remarks on Education, Trade Training, etc.: (Where and how was trade learned?)

FIRM EMPLOYEES SCHEDULE

(The information given will be regarded as confidential.)

Nature of business of firm......... ....

1. Total number of employees:

2. Total number Negro employees:

3. In spaces below state exact nature of work done by your Negro employees:

WORK DONE.	Male or F.	No. Employed.	Weekly Wages.	WORK DONE.	Male or F.	No. Employed.	Weekly Wages.

4. Are white workmen paid same wages for same kind of work?

5. Are your Negro workmen

   (a) Faster, equal, or slower in speed than white workmen?
       (*underline proper word*).

   (b) Better, equal, or poorer in quality of work done than white workmen?
       (*underline proper word*).

   (c) More, equally, or less reliable than white workmen?
       (*underline proper word*).

6. If not now, have you ever employed Negroes?

(See the other side.)

FIRM EMPLOYERS SCHEDULE (REVERSE SIDE)

7. If competent Negro workmen could be furnished, would you employ them?

8. If you would not employ them, please give reasons.

9. Remarks on attitude of your white workmen toward Negro workmen, etc.

BUSINESS SCHEDULE.

BUSINESS SCHEDULE—CONFIDENTIAL

FIRM NAME:

ADDRESS:

DATE:

WHEN ESTABLISHED: HOW LONG AT THIS ADDRESS?

INFORMANT:

1. Organization (underline): individual, partnership, number of partners.......... agent.

2. (underline): Manufacture, jobbing, wholesale, retail..........

3. Kind of service or goods offered (e. g., hotel, barber, groceries, real estate, etc.)

....

4. Number of employees:.......... Estimated total business done past 1907: $..........

1908: $..........

5. Previous occupations of owners or promoters:..........

6. Birthplace of owners or promoters:.......... Years in N. Y. City:..........

7. Valuation of plant, tools, fixtures, etc.: $.......... Of merchandise on hand: $..........

8. Other assets: $.......... Liabilities: $..........

9. Insurance: $.......... Rent per month: $.......... Floor space:..........

10. Nationality of customers:..........

11. Account books used (underline): Ledger, journal, cash-book, day-book..........

12. How often are books balanced?.......... 13 Inventory taken?..........

14. For what special reasons did you enter business: (How was capital secured?):..........

15. Remarks on history, etc., of firm: (Credit given occasionally? Habitually? Received?):..........

....

(For further remarks use back).

SELECT BIBLIOGRAPHY

Bibliography of the Negro American, Atlanta University Pub. no. 10. W. E. B. DuBois, editor, Atlanta, Ga., 1905.

Bibliography of Negroes. U. S. Congr. Lib., 324.

American Woman's Journal, July, 1895. The Story of an Old Wrong Atlanta University Publications, W. E. B. DuBois, editor.

No. 1. Mortality among Negroes in cities, pp. 51. Atlanta, Ga., 1896.

No. 3. Some efforts of American Negroes for their own social betterment, Atlanta Univ. Press, Atlanta, Ga., 1898, pp. 72.

No. 4. The Negro in Business, pp. 77, Atlanta, Ga., 1899.

Brackett, J. R. Status of the Slave, 1775-89. Johns Hopkins Univ. Studies.

Bulkley, William L. Industrial conditions of the Negro in New York. Annals, Amer. Acad., 27: 590-6. 1906.

Chapin, Robert Coit. Standards of living among workingmen's families in New York City. New York, 1909 (Russell Sage Foundation Publication).

Collin, G. L. A city within a city: St. Cyprian's parish. Outlook (N. Y.), 84: 274-7. 1906.

Colored Orphan Asylum and Association for Benefit of Colored Children. Annual reports, 1896—N. Y., 1896.

Commissioner of Education. Special report on the conditions of improvement of Public Schools in the D. of C., Washington, 1871, pp. 5-850, indices. (Schools of the Colored Population, pp. 193-400). U. S. Print.

Goodell, W. American Slave Code.

Griffin, Maude K. St. Mark's and its social work for Negroes. Charities, 15: 75-6. 1905.

Horsmanden, D. The New York conspiracy or history of the Negro Plot, New York, 1742.

Hansall, Geo. H. Reminiscences of New York Baptists.

Kellor, Frances A. Out of Work. A study of employment agencies, their treatment of the unemployed, and their influence upon homes and business. Knickerbocker Press, N. Y., 1904, pp. 283.

—— Southern colored girl in the North. Charities 13: 584-5. 1905.

154   [590

Laidlaw, Walter. Report of a sociological canvass of the Nineteenth Assembly District, 1897.

―――― The Federation of Churches and Christian workers in New York City. Canvasses: 1st, 112 pp.; 2nd, 116 pp., 1896.

Miller, Clifford L. The Negro students' summer vacation. Independent (N. Y.). June 16, 1904.

Morgan, E. V. Slavery in New York. American Historical Association, 1890.

More, Mrs. Louise Bolard. Wage-earners' budgets: Study of standards and cost of living in New York City. New York, 1907. 280 pp. (Greenwich House Series of Social Studies, No. 1.)

Minutes of the Common Council of the City of New York from 1675-1776. Published under the authority of the City of New York, by Dodd, Mead and Company. 1905. 8 vols.

Negro in the cities of the North, The. Articles by Lillian Brandt, Frances A. Kellor, Carl Kelsey, Booker T. Washington, William E. Benson, Mary W. Ovington, W. E. B. DuBois, John Daniels, Fannie B. Williams, etc. Charities 15:. 1, Oct., 1905.

New York (City) geneological and biological record.

New York Historical Society: Burghers and Freemen. New York collection of New York Historical Society for the year 1885. Publication Fund Series (Pub. in New York for the Society).

Ovington, Mary White. The Negro home in New York. Charities 15: 25-30, 1905.

――――The Negro in trades unions in New York City. Annals Amer. Acad., 27: 551-558, 1906.

――――Fresh-air work among Colored children in New York. Charities, 17: 115-7, 1906.

―――― Half a Man. New York, 1911. 227 pp.

O'Callahan, E. B. Documents relative to the Colonial history of New York state. Procured in Holland, England and France by John Romeyn Brodhead, Esq. (Published by Weid Parsons and Company. Vols. i. and ii. Albany, 1856.

―――― Laws and Ordinances of New Netherland, 1638-1674. Compiled and translated from the original Dutch records in the office of the Secretary of State, Albany, N. Y. (Published by Weid Parsons and Company, 1868.)

Pelletreau, William S. Historic homes and institutions and geneological and family histories of New York. 4 vols. N. Y., 1907. Illustrated.

Pratt, E. E. Industrial causes of congestion of population in N. Y. City. pp. 260. N. Y., 1911. (No. 109 of the Columbia University Series in History, Economics and Public Law.)

Proceedings of the Grand Lodge of Free and Accepted Masons of New York.

Proceedings of the Select Committee of the United States Senate. Investigation into the cases of the removal of Negroes from the Southern states into the Northern states. 3 Parts. 1,486 pp. 2 vols. Washington.

Speed, J. G. Negroes in New York. Harpers' Weekly, 44: 1249-50.

Scottron, Samuel R. The Negro in business before the war. Colored American Magazine, October, 1907.

Thompson, Mary W. Sketches of the History, character and dying testimony of beneficiaries of the Colored Home in the City of New York. pp. 3-78. N. Y., 1851.

Tucker, Helen A. Negro craftsman in New York. Southern Workman, 36: 545-551. 1907; 37: 1.

Tyler, Edith. New York settlement for Negroes. The Stillman Branch of the Henery Street Settlement. Charities, 18: 328. 1907.

United States, Twelfth Census, Special Report: Employees and Wages.

────── Bulletin 8, Negroes in the United States.

────── Women at Work.

Wheller, B. F. The Varrick Family.

Williams, G. W. History of the Negro race in America from 1619-1880. Negroes as slaves, as soldiers, and as citizens. 2 vols. N. Y., 1883.

INDEX